Learning QGIS 2.0

Use QGIS to create great maps and perform
all the geoprocessing tasks you need

Anita Graser

BIRMINGHAM - MUMBAI

Learning QGIS 2.0

First published: September 2013

Production Reference: 1100913

Published by Packt Publishing Ltd.
Livery Place
35 Livery Street
Birmingham B3 2PB, UK.

ISBN 978-1-78216-748-8

www.packtpub.com

Cover Image by Suresh Mogre (suresh.mogre.99@gmail.com)

Credits

Author
Anita Graser

Reviewers
Werner Macho
Nathan Woodrow

Acquisition Editor
Kevin Colaco

Commissioning Editor
Sharvari Tawde

Technical Editor
Sonali S. Vernekar

Copy Editors
Aditya Nair
Alfida Paiva
Laxmi Subramanian

Project Coordinator
Esha Thakker

Proofreader
Paul Hindle

Indexer
Priya Subramani

Graphics
Ronak Dhruv

Production Coordinator
Manu Joseph

Cover Work
Manu Joseph

About the Author

Anita Graser studied at FH Wr. Neustadt, Austria, where she graduated with a Master's degree in Geomatics in 2010. During her studies, she acquired hands-on experience in the fields of geomarketing and transportation research. Since 2007, Anita has been working as a geographic information systems (GIS) expert with the Dynamic Transportation Systems group at the Austrian Institute of Technology, where she focuses on analyzing and visualizing spatio-temporal data and research project management. Anita is an OSGeo Charter member and QGIS team member. She has been working with GIS since 2005, and is writing a popular blog on open source GIS at `anitagraser.com`.

Special thanks go to Werner Macho and Nathan Woodrow for their valuable feedback and support while writing this book. I would also like to thank my family, partner, and coworkers for their support and encouragement. And of course, I want to thank the whole QGIS team for their continued effort to provide the best open source GIS experience possible.

About the Reviewers

Werner Macho completed his Master's degree at the University of Natural Resources and Life Sciences, Vienna, Austria. There he spent a long period of time as a scientist working on a range of topics. Currently, he is completing his second Master's degree in GIS Science at the University of Salzburg, Austria, while working at linfiniti.com in Swellendam, South Africa. Werner has been working with QGIS since 2007, when he searched for an open source GIS tool to aid in his work on floodwater protection plans. In the QGIS Project, he holds the position of Translation Team Leader, managing the translation of more than 45 languages. Werner also banned proprietary stuff from his computer in 1995, and he strongly believes in the power of coding open source and the GPL.

Nathan Woodrow is an open source developer working on the QGIS project, he also maintains a collection of his own personal open source projects. Nathan has been a core developer and an active member of the QGIS community for the last three years. Nathan maintains a QGIS blog at `http://nathanw.net` which showcases some of the upcoming features in QGIS, as well as tips and tricks for developers and users.

Nathan currently works for Digital Mapping Solutions (DMS) Australia, as a Technical Consultant and QGIS Specialist. At DMS Nathan provides support, training, custom development, and bug fixing for QGIS.

www.PacktPub.com

Support files, eBooks, discount offers and more

You might want to visit www.PacktPub.com for support files and downloads related to your book.

Did you know that Packt offers eBook versions of every book published, with PDF and ePub files available? You can upgrade to the eBook version at www.PacktPub.com and as a print book customer, you are entitled to a discount on the eBook copy. Get in touch with us at service@packtpub.com for more details.

At www.PacktPub.com, you can also read a collection of free technical articles, sign up for a range of free newsletters and receive exclusive discounts and offers on Packt books and eBooks.

http://PacktLib.PacktPub.com

Do you need instant solutions to your IT questions? PacktLib is Packt's online digital book library. Here, you can access, read and search across Packt's entire library of books.

Why Subscribe?
* Fully searchable across every book published by Packt
* Copy and paste, print and bookmark content
* On demand and accessible via web browser

Free Access for Packt account holders

If you have an account with Packt at www.PacktPub.com, you can use this to access PacktLib today and view nine entirely free books. Simply use your login credentials for immediate access.

Table of Contents

Preface

Welcome to *Learning QGIS 2.0*. This book aims to introduce you to QGIS 2 and how to perform core geospatial tasks using this popular open source GIS. It takes you through five chapters, from QGIS installation and setup in the first chapter, to the essentials of viewing spatial data in the second chapter. The third chapter covers data creation and editing, followed by the fourth chapter, which offers an introduction to performing spatial analysis in QGIS. In the final chapter, you will learn how to create great maps and how to prepare them for print.

What this book covers

Chapter 1, Getting Started with QGIS, covers the installation and configuration of QGIS. We will also get to know the user interface and how to customize it. By the end of this chapter, you will have QGIS running on your machine and be ready to start with the tutorials.

Chapter 2, Viewing Spatial Data, covers how to view spatial data from different data sources. QGIS supports many file and database formats as well as OGC web services. We will first see how we can load layers from these different data sources. Then, we will look into the basics of styling both vector and raster layers and will create our first map. We will finish this chapter with an example for loading background maps from online services.

Chapter 3, Data Creation and Editing, covers the creation of new vector layers. Then, we will cover how to select features and take measurements before we continue with editing feature geometries and attributes. We will then reproject vector and raster data and learn how to convert between different file formats before we end this chapter with joining data from text files and spreadsheets to our spatial data.

Chapter 4, Spatial Analysis, covers raster processing and analysis tasks such as clipping and terrain analysis. Then, we cover converting between raster and vector formats before we continue with common vector geoprocessing tasks such as generating heatmaps and calculating area shares within a region. Finally, we will finish the chapter with an exercise in automating a geoprocessing workflow using the QGIS Processing modeler.

Chapter 5, Creating Great Maps, covers important features that enable us to create great maps. We will go into advanced vector styling, building on what we learned in *Chapter 2, Viewing Spatial Data.* Then, we will cover labeling using examples of labeling point locations as well as creating more advanced road labels with road shield graphics. We will also cover how to tweak labels manually. Finally, we will get to know the print composer and how to use it to create printable maps and map books.

Who this book is for

This book is for users, developers, and consultants who know the basic functions and processes of GIS, but want to know how to use QGIS to achieve the results they are used to from other GIS. This book is not intended to be a GIS textbook. The reader is expected to be comfortable with core GIS concepts.

Conventions

In this book, you will find a number of styles of text that distinguish between different kinds of information. Here are some examples of these styles, and an explanation of their meaning.

Code words in text are shown as follows: "use [% $now %] to insert the current time stamp."

A block of code is set as follows:

```
( landcover@1 > 0 AND landcover@1 <= 6 ) * 100
+ ( landcover@1 >= 7 AND landcover@1 <= 10 ) * 101
+ ( landcover@1 >= 11 ) * 102
```

Any command-line input or output is written as follows:

```
sudo apt-get install qgis python-qgis qgis-plugin-grass
```

New terms and **important words** are shown in bold. Words that you see on the screen, in menus or dialog boxes for example, appear in the text like this: "clicking the **Next** button moves you to the next screen".

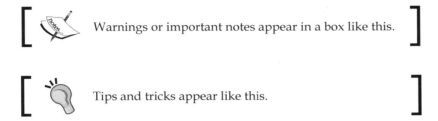

Warnings or important notes appear in a box like this.

Tips and tricks appear like this.

Reader feedback

Feedback from our readers is always welcome. Let us know what you think about this book—what you liked or may have disliked. Reader feedback is important for us to develop titles that you really get the most out of.

To send us general feedback, simply send an e-mail to feedback@packtpub.com, and mention the book title via the subject of your message.

If there is a topic that you have expertise in and you are interested in either writing or contributing to a book, see our author guide on www.packtpub.com/authors.

Customer support

Now that you are the proud owner of a Packt book, we have a number of things to help you to get the most from your purchase.

Errata

Although we have taken every care to ensure the accuracy of our content, mistakes do happen. If you find a mistake in one of our books—maybe a mistake in the text or the code—we would be grateful if you would report this to us. By doing so, you can save other readers from frustration and help us improve subsequent versions of this book. If you find any errata, please report them by visiting http://www.packtpub.com/submit-errata, selecting your book, clicking on the **errata submission form** link, and entering the details of your errata. Once your errata are verified, your submission will be accepted and the errata will be uploaded on our website, or added to any list of existing errata, under the Errata section of that title. Any existing errata can be viewed by selecting your title from http://www.packtpub.com/support.

Piracy

Piracy of copyrighted material on the Internet is an ongoing problem across all media. At Packt, we take the protection of our copyright and licenses very seriously. If you come across any illegal copies of our works, in any form, on the Internet, please provide us with the location address or website name immediately so that we can pursue a remedy.

Please contact us at copyright@packtpub.com with a link to the suspected pirated material.

We appreciate your help in protecting our authors, and our ability to bring you valuable content.

Questions

You can contact us at questions@packtpub.com if you are having a problem with any aspect of the book, and we will do our best to address it.

Getting Started with QGIS

1

In this chapter, we will install and configure the QGIS geographic information system. We will also get to know the user interface and how to customize it. By the end of this chapter, you will have QGIS running on your machine and be ready to start with the tutorials.

Installing QGIS

QGIS runs on Windows, various Linux distributions, Unix, Mac OS X, and Android. Also, the QGIS Project provides ready-to-use packages as well as instructions for building from source code on `download.qgis.org`. We will cover how to install QGIS on the two most common systems, Windows and Ubuntu, as well as how to avoid the most common pitfalls.

Like many other open source projects, QGIS offers you a choice between a stable release version and the cutting-edge developer version, also called **master**. QGIS master will contain the latest and greatest developments, but be warned that on some days, it might not work as reliably as you are used to. For the tutorials in this book, we will be using the QGIS 2.0 release.

Installing on Windows

On Windows, we have two different options to install QGIS: standalone installer and OSGeo4W installer. The standalone installer is one big download (approximately of 130 MB), which contains a QGIS release and the **Geographic Resources Analysis Support System (GRASS)** GIS in one package. The OSGeo4W installer is a small, flexible installation tool that makes it possible to download and install QGIS and many more OSGeo tools with all their dependencies. The main advantage of this over the standalone installer is that it makes updating QGIS and its dependencies very easy. You can always have access to both the current release and the developer version, if you chose so, but of course, you are never forced to update. That's why I recommend using OSGeo4W. The OSGeo4W installer can be downloaded from osgeo4w.osgeo.org (or directly from download.osgeo.org/osgeo4w/osgeo4w-setup.exe). Download it and keep it! In the future, whenever you want to change or update your system, just run it again.

 Regardless of the installer you choose, make sure to avoid special characters in the installation path, as they can cause problems later on, for example, during plugin installation.

When the OSGeo4W installer starts, we get to choose between the **Express Desktop**, **Express Web-GIS**, and **Advanced** installation. To install the QGIS release version, we can simply select the **Express Desktop** option and the next dialog will list the available desktop applications such as QGIS, uDig, and GRASS GIS. We simply select QGIS, click on **Next** and download and installation will start automatically. When the installation has finished, there will be desktop shortcuts and start menu entries for OSGeo4W and QGIS.

If we want to install QGIS master, we need to go through the **Advanced** installation. This installation path offers many options such as **Download without installing** and **Install from Local Directory**, which can be used to download all the necessary packages on one machine to later install them on machines without Internet access. It's usually not necessary to change the default settings, but if your machine is, for example, hidden behind a proxy, you will be able to specify it here. After the installer fetches the latest package information from OSGeo's servers, we get to pick the packages for installation. QGIS master is listed in the desktop category as **qgis-dev**. To select it for installation, click on the text that reads **Skip** and it will change and display the version number. The installer will automatically select all the necessary dependencies (such as GDAL, SAGA, OTB, and GRASS), so we don't have to worry about that. After clicking on **Next**, the download and installation starts automatically just like in the Express version. The dialog will look like the following screenshot:

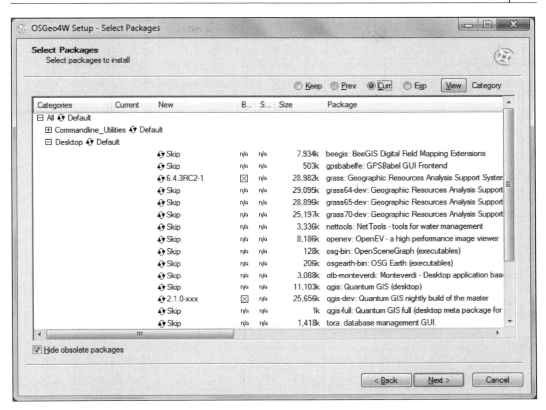

If you try to run QGIS and get a pop up saying **The procedure entry point <some-name> could not be located in the dynamic link library <dll-name>.dll**, you are facing a common issue on Windows systems: a DLL conflict. They are easy to fix; just copy the DLL file mentioned in the error message from C:\OSGeo4W\bin\ to C:\OSGeo4W\apps\qgis\bin\ (adjust paths if necessary).

Installing on Ubuntu

On Ubuntu, the QGIS project provides packages for both the release and developer version. Be aware, though, that you can only install one version at a time. The packages are not listed in the default Ubuntu repositories. Therefore, we have to add the appropriate repositories to Ubuntu's sources list, which you can find in /etc/apt/sources.list. You can open the file with any text editor.

Make sure that you have super user rights, as you need them to save your edits. One option is to use gedit, which is installed on Ubuntu by default. To edit the sources.list file, use the following command:

```
sudo gedit /etc/apt/sources.list
```

Make sure to add only one of the following four package source options to avoid conflicts due to incompatible packages. The specific lines you have to add to the source list depend on your Ubuntu version.

The first and default option is to install the current release version. To install the QGIS release on Precise Penguin, add the following lines to your file:

```
deb      http://qgis.org/debian precise main
deb-src http://qgis.org/debian precise main
```

If necessary, replace precise with raring, oneiric, natty, or lucid to fit your system. For an updated list of supported Ubuntu versions, check download.qgis.org.

The second option is to install the QGIS master, which is currently available for precise, quantal, and raring. Add the following lines to your file:

```
deb      http://qgis.org/debian-nightly precise main
deb-src http://qgis.org/debian-nightly precise main
```

 The preceding versions depend on other packages such as GDAL and proj4, which are available in the Ubuntu repositories. It is worth mentioning that these packages are often quite old.

Therefore, the third option is to install the QGIS release version with updated dependencies, which are provided by the ubuntugis repository. Add the following lines to your file:

```
deb      http://ppa.launchpad.net/ubuntugis/ubuntugis-unstable/ubuntu
precise main
deb-src http://ppa.launchpad.net/ubuntugis/ubuntugis-unstable/ubuntu
precise main
```

The fourth option is QGIS master with updated dependencies. Add the following lines to your file:

```
deb      http://qgis.org/ubuntugis-nightly precise main
deb-src http://qgis.org/ubuntugis-nightly precise main
deb      http://ppa.launchpad.net/ubuntugis/ubuntugis-unstable/ubuntu
precise main
```

After choosing the repository, we add the `qgis.org` repository public key to our `apt` keyring. This will avoid warnings you might otherwise get when installing from a non-default repository. Run the following command in the terminal:

```
gpg --keyserver keyserver.ubuntu.com --recv 997D3880

gpg --export --armor 997D3880 | sudo apt-key add -
```

> The key information might have changed since this book went into print. Please refer to `hub.qgis.org/projects/quantum-gis/wiki/Download#26-Ubuntu` for the latest updates.

Finally, to install QGIS, run the following commands:

```
sudo apt-get update
sudo apt-get install qgis python-qgis qgis-plugin-grass
```

Running QGIS for the first time

By default, QGIS will use the operating system's default language. To follow the tutorials in this book, it is advisable to change the language to English by navigating to **Settings | Options | Locale**. On the first run, the toolbars are arranged in two rows and depending on your screen resolution, this can hide many buttons. To be able to work efficiently, I therefore suggest arranging the toolbars. I like to put some toolbars to the left and right screen borders to save vertical screen estate—especially on wide-screen displays.

Additionally, we activate the file browser by navigating to **View** | **Panels** | **Browser**. It will provide us quick access to our spatial data. In the end, your screen should look similar to the following screenshot:

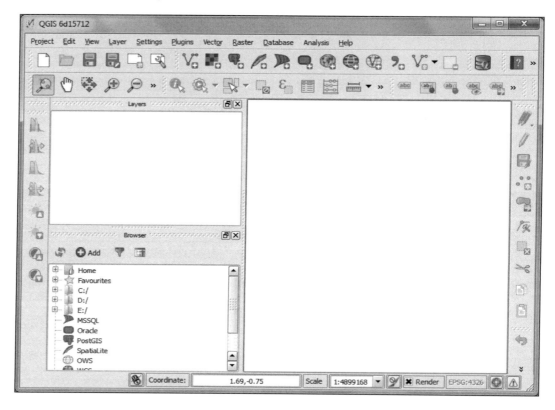

Next, we activate some must-have plugins by navigating to **Plugins** | **Manage and Install Plugins**. Plugins are activated by ticking the checkbox beside their name. To begin with, I recommend the following:

- **Coordinate Capture**: This plugin is useful for picking coordinates in the map
- **fTools**: This plugin offers vector analysis and management tools
- **GdalTools**: This plugin offers raster analysis and management tools
- **Processing**: This plugin provides access to many useful raster and vector analysis tools as well as a model builder for task automation

To make it easier to find specific plugins, we can filter the list of plugins using the **Search** input field at the top of the window, which you can see in the following screenshot:

Introducing the QGIS user interface

Now that we have set up QGIS, let's get accustomed to the interface! The biggest area is reserved for the map. To the left of the map, there are the **Layers** and the **Browser** panels. Below the map, we find important information such as (from left to right), current map coordinates, map scale, and the (currently inactive) project **coordinate reference system** (**CRS**).

Next, there are multiple toolbars to explore. If you arranged them as shown in the previous section, you'll find the following toolbars in the top row:

- **File**: This toolbar contains tools to create, open, save, and print projects
- **Manage Layers**: This toolbar contains tools to add layers from vector or raster files, databases, web services, text files, or create new layers

- **Database**: Currently, this toolbar only contains DB Manager, but other database-related tools will appear here when they are installed
- **Help**: This points to the user manual download

The following screenshot shows what the preceding toolbars look like:

The second row of toolbars contains the following:

- **Map Navigation**: This toolbar contains pan and zoom tools
- **Attributes**: These tools are used to identify, select, open attribute tables, measure, and so on
- **Label**: These tools are used to add, configure, and modify labels
- **Vector**: This is currently empty, but will be filled by additional Python plugins
- **Web**: This is currently empty, but will be filled by additional Python plugins

The following screenshot shows what the preceding toolbars look like:

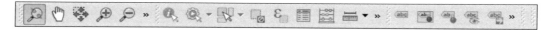

On the left screen border, we put the following:

- **Plugins**: This is currently empty, but will be filled by additional Python plugins
- **Raster**: This toolbar includes histogram stretch, brightness, and contrast control

The following screenshot shows what the preceding toolbars look like:

Finally, on the right screen border, we find the following:

- **Digitizing**: These tools enable editing, basic feature creation, and editing
- **Advanced Digitizing**: This toolbar contains undo/redo, advanced editing tools, geometry simplification, and so on

The following screenshot shows what the preceding toolbars look like:

All digitizing tools are currently inactive. They will only turn active once we start editing a vector layer.

Toolbars and panels can be activated and deactivated via the **View** menu's **Panels** and **Toolbars** entries as well as by right-clicking on a menu or toolbar, which opens a context menu with all available toolbars and panels. All toolbar tools can also be accessed via the menu. If you deactivate the **Manage Layers** toolbar, for example, you will still be able to add layers using the **Layer** menu.

QGIS is highly customizable. You can increase your productivity by assigning shortcuts to the tools you use regularly by navigating to **Settings | Configure shortcuts**. Similarly, if you find that you never use a certain toolbar button or menu entry, you can hide it by navigating to **Settings | Customization**. For example, if you don't have access to an Oracle Spatial database, you might want to hide the associated buttons to remove clutter and save screen estate as shown in the following screenshot:

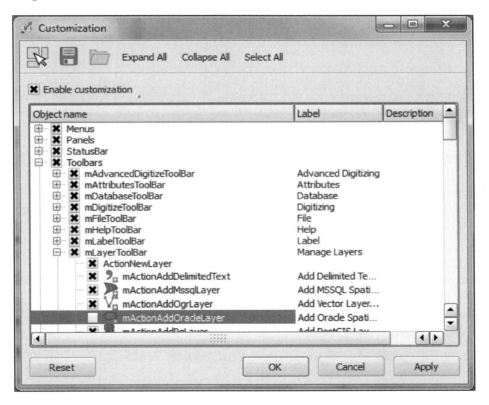

Summary

In this chapter, we installed QGIS and configured it by selecting useful defaults and arranging the user interface elements. Finally, we explored the panels, toolbars, and menus that make up the QGIS user interface, and learned how to customize them to increase productivity.

2
Viewing Spatial Data

In this chapter, we will cover how to view spatial data from different data sources. QGIS supports many file and database formats as well as OGC Web Services. We will first see how we can load layers from these different data sources. We will then look into the basics of styling both vector and raster layers and will create our first map, which you can see in the following screenshot. We will finish this chapter with an example for loading background maps from online services.

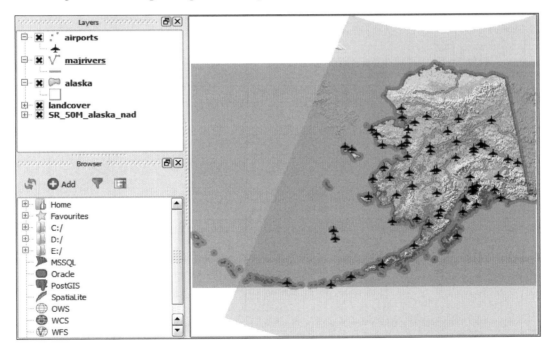

For the examples in this chapter, we will be using sample data provided by the QGIS project and available for download from `download.osgeo.org/qgis/data/qgis_sample_data.zip` (20 MB). Download and unzip it.

Loading vector data from files

In this section, we will talk about loading vector data from GIS formats such as Shapefiles as well as from text files.

We can load vector files using the menu entry by going to **Layer | Add vector layer** and also by using the **Add vector layer** toolbar button. If you like shortcuts, use *Ctrl + Shift + V*. In the **Add vector layer** dialog, we find a drop-down list that allows us to specify the encoding of the input file. This option is important if we are dealing with files that contain special characters, such as German umlauts or letters from alphabets other than the default Latin one. The following screenshot shows the **Add vector layer** dialog:

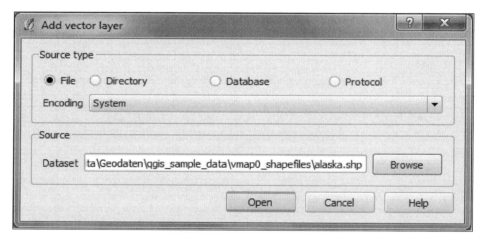

What we are most interested in now is the **Browse** button, which opens the file-opening dialog. Note the **file type filter** drop-down list on the bottom-right corner of the dialog. We can open it to see a list of the supported vector file types. This filter is useful to find specific files faster by hiding all files of a different type, but be aware that the filter settings are stored and will be applied again the next time we open the dialog.

This can be a source of confusion if we later try to find a different file and it happens to be hidden by the filter, so remember to check the filter settings if you are having trouble locating a file.

We can load more than one file in one go by selecting multiple files at once (holding down *Ctrl* on Windows/Ubuntu or *Cmd* on Mac). Let's give it a try.

1. We select `alaska.shp` and `airports.shp` from the sample data `vmap0_shapefiles` folder.

2. Next, we confirm our selection by clicking on **Open**, and we are taken back to the **Add vector layer** dialog.

3. After clicking on **Open** once more, the selected files are loaded. You will notice that each vector layer is displayed in a random color. Don't worry about that now. We'll deal with layer styles later in this chapter.

There are multiple tricks that make loading data even faster; for example, you can simply drag and drop files from the operating system file browser into QGIS. Another way to quickly access your spatial data is by using QGIS' built-in file browser. If you set up QGIS as shown in *Chapter 1, Getting Started with QGIS*, you'll find the browser on the left-hand side, just below the layer list. Navigate to your data folder and you can again drag and drop files from the browser to the map. Additionally, you can mark a folder as favorite by right-clicking on the folder and selecting **Add to favorites**. This way, your data folders will be even faster to access because they are added in the **Favorites** section right at the top of the browser list.

Another popular source of spatial data are delimited text (CSV) files. QGIS can load CSV files using the **Add Delimited Text Layer** option available via the menu entry by going to **Layers | Add Delimited Text Layer** or the corresponding toolbar button. Click on **Browse** and select `elevp.csv` from the sample data. CSVs come with all kinds of delimiters. As you can see in the following screenshot, the plugin lets you choose from the most common ones (**Comma, Tab**, and so on), but you can also specify any other plain or regular expression delimiter. If your CSV contains quotation marks such as " or ', you can use the **Quote** option to have them removed. The **Number of header lines to discard** option allows us to skip extra lines at the beginning of the text file. The following **Field options** include functionality to trim extra spaces from field values or to redefine the decimal separator to a comma. The spatial information itself can be provided either in two columns containing coordinates of points X and Y or by using the **Well known text (WKT)** format. A WKT field can contain points, lines, or polygons.

WKT is a very useful and flexible format. For example, a line can be specified by writing `LINESTRING (30 10, 10 30, 40 40)`. If you are unfamiliar with the concept, you can find an introduction with examples at `en.wikipedia.org/wiki/Well-known_text`.

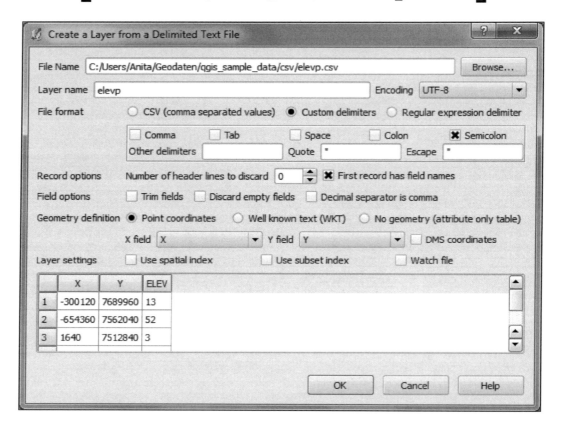

After clicking on **OK**, QGIS will prompt us to specify the layer's **coordinate reference system (CRS)**. We will talk about handling coordinate reference systems next.

Dealing with coordinate reference systems

Whenever we load a data source, QGIS looks for usable CRS information; for example, in the Shapefile's `.prj` file. If QGIS cannot find any usable information, it will by default ask you to specify the CRS manually. This behavior can be changed by going to **Settings | Options | CRS** to always use either the project CRS or a default CRS.

The QGIS Coordinate Reference System Selector offers a filter that makes finding the CRS easier. It can filter by name or by ID (for example, the EPSG code). Just start typing and watch how the list of potential CRSs gets shorter. There are actually two separate lists: the upper one contains the CRSs we have recently used while the lower list is much longer and contains all available CRSs. For the `elevp.csv` file, we select **NAD27 / Alaska Albers**.

If we want to check a layer's CRS, we can find this information in the layer properties' **General** section, which can be accessed by going to **Layer | Properties** or by double-clicking on the layer name in the layer list. If you think that QGIS picked the wrong CRS or you made a mistake specifying the CRS, you can correct the CRS settings using **Specify CRS**. Note that this does not change the underlying data or reproject it. We'll talk about reprojecting vectors and raster files in *Chapter 3, Data Creation and Editing*.

In QGIS, we can create a map out of multiple layers even if each dataset is stored with a different CRS. QGIS handles the necessary reprojections automatically by enabling a mechanism called on-the-fly reprojection, which can be accessed by going to **Settings | Project Properties** as you can see in the following screenshot:

All layers are reprojected to the project CRS on the fly, which means that QGIS calculates these reprojections dynamically and only for the purpose of rendering the map. The underlying data is not changed and spatial analyses are not affected.

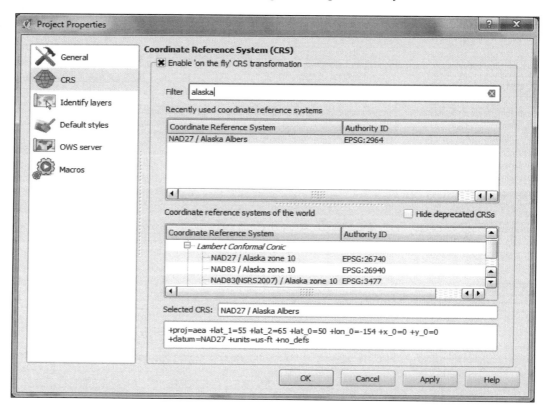

In some cases, you might have to specify a CRS that is not available in QGIS' CRS database. You can add CRS definitions by going to **Settings | Custom CRS**. Click on the **Add new CRS** button to create a new entry, type in a name for the new CRS, and paste the proj4 definition string. Just close the dialog by clicking on **OK** when you are done.

Loading raster files

Loading raster files is not much different from loading vector files. Selecting the menu entry **Layer** and then clicking on **Add Raster Layer**, clicking on the **Add Raster Layer** button, or pressing the *Ctrl + Shift + R* shortcut will take you directly to the file-opening dialog. Again, you can check the file type filter to see a list of supported file types.

Let's give it a try and load `landcover.img` from the sample data `raster` folder. Similarly, just like vector files, you can load rasters by dragging them into QGIS from the operating system or the built-in file browser.

> Support for all these different vector and raster file types in QGIS is handled by the powerful GDAL/OGR package. You can check the full list of supported formats at `www.gdal.org/formats_list.html` (for rasters) and `www.gdal.org/ogr/ogr_formats.html` (for vectors).

Georeferencing raster maps

Some raster data sources, such as simple scanned maps, lack proper spatial referencing, and we have to georeference them before we can use them in a GIS. In QGIS, we can georeference rasters using the Georeferencer GDAL plugin, which can be accessed by going to **Raster | Georeferencer** (enable it by going to **Plugins | Manage and Install Plugins** if you cannot find it in the **Raster** menu).

Georeferencer covers the following use cases:

- We can create a world file for a raster file without altering the original raster.
- If we have a map image that contains points with known coordinates, we can set **ground control points** (**GCPs**) and enter the known coordinates.
- Finally, if we don't know the coordinates of any points on the map, we still have the chance to place GCPs manually using a second, already georeferenced map of the same area. We can use objects that are visible in both maps to pick points in the map that we want to georeference and work out their coordinates from the reference map.

After loading a raster into Georeferencer by going to **File | Open raster** or using the **Open raster** toolbar button, we are asked to specify the CRS of the ground control points we are planning to add. Next, we can start adding ground control points by going to **Edit | Add point**. We can use the pan and zoom tools to navigate and we can place GCPs by clicking on the map. We are then prompted to insert the coordinates of the new point or pick them from the reference map in the main QGIS window.

After placing the GCPs, we can define the transformation algorithm by going to **Settings | Transformation Settings**. Which algorithm you choose depends on your input data and the level of geometric distortion you want to allow. The most commonly used algorithms are polynomial 1 to 3. A first-order polynomial transformation allows scaling, translation, and rotation only.

A second-order polynomial transformation can handle some curvature, and a third-order polynomial transformation consequently allows for even higher degrees of distortion. The thin-plate spline algorithm can handle local deformations in the map, and is therefore very useful when working with very low-quality map scans. The linear option, on the other hand, is only used to create world files, and as mentioned previously, this does not actually transform the raster.

The resampling method depends on your input data and the result you want to achieve. Cubic resampling creates smooth results, but if you don't want to change the raster values, choose the nearest neighbor method.

Before we can start the georeferencing process, we still have to specify the output file name and target CRS. Make sure that the **Load in QGIS when done** option is active. Then, we can close the **Transformation Settings** dialog and go to **File | Start Georeferencing**. The georeferenced raster will automatically be loaded into the QGIS main map window.

Loading data from databases

QGIS supports PostGIS, SpatiaLite, MSSQL, SQL Anywhere, and Oracle Spatial databases. We will cover the two open source options: PostGIS and SpatiaLite. Both are available cross-platform, just like QGIS.

SpatiaLite is the spatial extension for Sqlite databases. Sqlite is a self-contained, serverless, zero-configuration, transactional SQL database engine (www.sqlite.org). This basically means that an Sqlite database, and therefore also a SpatiaLite database, doesn't need a server installation, and can be copied and exchanged just like any ordinary file.

You can download an example database from www.gaia-gis.it/spatialite-2.3.1/test-2.3.zip. Unzip the file; you will be able to connect to it by going to **Layer | Add SpatiaLite Layer**, using the **Add SpatiaLite Layer** toolbar button, or by pressing *Ctrl + Shift + L*. Click on **New** to select the database file test-2.3.sqlite. QGIS will save all connections and add them to the drop-down list at the top. After clicking on **Connect**, you will see the list of layers stored in the database as shown in the following screenshot:

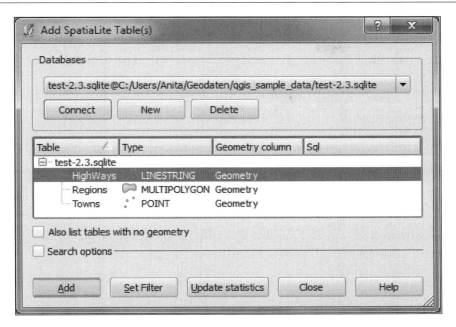

Like with files, you can select one or more tables from the list and click on **Add** to load them into the map. Additionally, you can use **Set Filter** to load only specific features.

Filters in QGIS use SQL-like syntax; for example, `"Name" = 'EMILIA-ROMAGNA'` to select only the region called EMILIA-ROMAGNA, or `"Name" LIKE 'ISOLA%'` to select all regions starting with ISOLA. The filter queries are passed on to the underlying data provider (for example, Spatialite or OGR). The provider syntax for basic filter queries is consistent over different providers, but can vary when using more exotic functions. You can read up on the details of OGR SQL on `http://www.gdal.org/ogr/ogr_sql.html`.

PostGIS is the spatial extension for the PostgreSQL database system. Installing and configuring the database is out of the scope of this book, but there are installers for Windows and packages for many Linux distributions as well as for Mac. To load data from a PostGIS database, go to **Layers** | **Add PostGIS Layer**, use the **Add PostGIS Layer** toolbar button, or press *Ctrl + Shift + D*.

When using a database for the first time, click on **New** to establish a new database connection. In the following dialog, you can specify a **Name** for the new connection. Other fields that have to be filled are as follows:

- **Host**: The server's IP address is inserted in this field. You can use localhost if PostGIS is running locally.
- **Port**: The PostGIS default port is 5432.
- **Database**: This is the name of the PostGIS database you want to connect to.
- **Username** and **Password**: For convenience, you can tell QGIS to save them.

The following screenshot shows the dialog to create a new connection to a database called **postgis**:

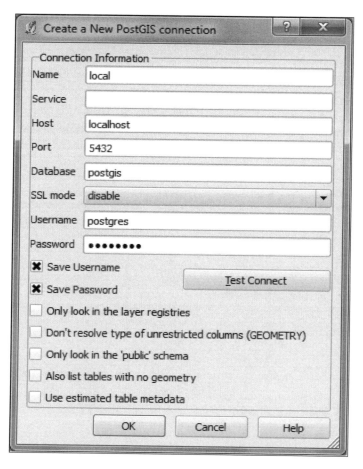

After the connection is established, you can load and filter tables just like we discussed for SpatiaLite.

Loading data from web services

More and more data providers offer access to their datasets via OGC-compliant web services such as WMS, WCS, or WFS. QGIS supports these services out-of-the-box.

You can load WMS layers by going to **Layer | Add WMS Layer**, by clicking on the **Add WMS Layer** button, or by pressing *Ctrl + Shift + W*. If you know a WMS server, you can connect to it by clicking on **New** and filling in a name and the URL. All other fields are optional. Don't worry if you don't know of any WMS server, because we can simply click on **Add default servers** to get access information about servers whose administrators collaborate with the QGIS project. One of these servers is called **Lizardtech server**. Select it, or any of the other servers, from the drop-down box and click on **Connect** to see the list of layers available through the server.

From the layer list, you can now select one or more layers for download. It is worth noting that the order in which you select the layers does matter because the layers will be combined on the server side, and QGIS will only receive the combined image as the resultant layer. If you want to be able to use the layers separately, you have to download them one by one. The data download starts once you click on **Add**. The dialog will stay open so that you can add additional layers from the server.

Many WMS servers offer their layers in multiple different CRSs. You can check the list of available CRSs by clicking on the **Change** button at the bottom of the dialog. This will open a CRS selector dialog, which is limited to the WMS server's CRS capabilities.

Loading data from WCS or WFS servers works in the same way, but public servers are rare and unreliable, and therefore no recommendation can be provided here.

Styling raster layers

After this introduction to data sources, we can now create our first map. We will build the map from the bottom up by first loading some background rasters (hillshade and land cover), which we will then overlay with point, line, and polygon layers.

Let's start by loading land cover and hillshade from `landcover.img` and `SR_50M_alaska_nad.tif` and then opening the **Style** section in layer properties (**Layer | Properties** or by double-clicking on the layer name). QGIS tries to pick a reasonable default render type. The hillshade raster, `SR_50M_alaska_nad.tif`, is loaded with the **Singleband gray** render type as you can see in the following screenshot. If we want to render the hillshade raster in color instead of grayscale, we can change the render type to **Singleband pseudocolor**. In pseudocolor mode, we can create color maps either manually or by selecting one of the premade color ramps. But let's stick with **Singleband gray** for hillshade for now.

Below the color settings, we find a section with more advanced options that control raster resampling, brightness, contrast, saturation, and hue—options you probably know from image processing software. By default, resampling is set to the fast **Nearest neighbour** option. To get nice, smoother results, we can change to the **Bilinear** or **Cubic** method.

Click on **Ok** or **Apply** to confirm. In both cases, the map will be redrawn using the new layer style. If you click on **Apply**, the **Layer Properties** dialog stays open and you can continue to fine-tune the layer style. If you click on **Ok**, the **Layer Properties** dialog is closed.

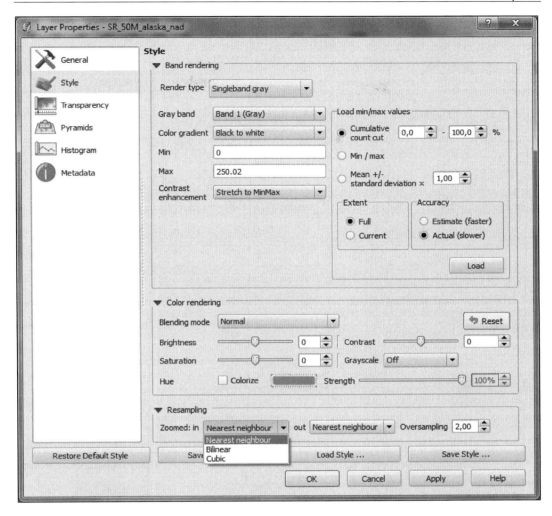

The `landcover.img` raster is a good example of a paletted raster. Each cell value is mapped to a specific color. To change a color, we can simply double-click on the **Color** preview and a color picker will open.

The style section of a paletted raster looks like the following screenshot:

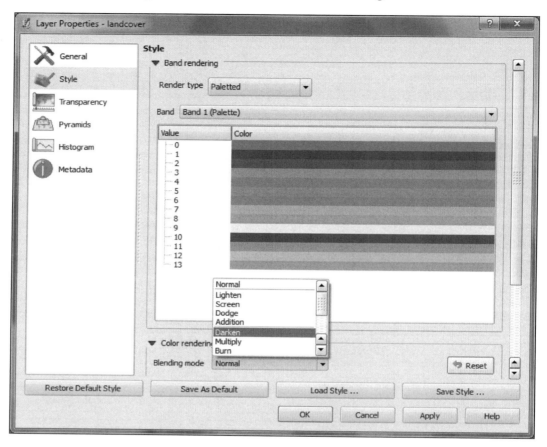

If we want to combine hillshade and land cover into one aesthetically pleasing background, we can use a combination of the **Blending mode** and layer **Transparency**. Blending modes are another feature commonly found in image-processing software. The main advantage of blending modes over transparency is that we can avoid the usually dull, low-contrast look that results from combining rasters using transparency alone. If you haven't had any experience with blending, take some time to try the different effects. For this example, I used the **Darken** blending mode, as highlighted in the previous screenshot, together with a global layer transparency of **50 %,** as shown in the following screenshot:

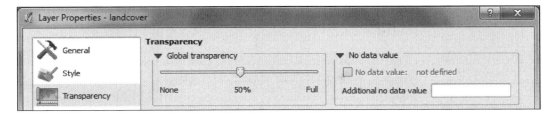

Styling vector layers

When we load vector layers, QGIS renders them using a default style and a random color. Of course, we want to customize these styles to better reflect our data. In the following exercises, we will style point, line, and polygon layers, and we will also get accustomed with the most common vector styling options.

Creating point styles – an example of an airport style

Let's get started with a point layer! Load `airport.shp` from our sample data. Regardless of the layer's geometry type, we always find a drop-down list with the available style options in the upper-left corner of the **Style** dialog.

The following style options are available for vector layers:

- **Single Symbol**: This is the simplest option. When we use a Single Symbol style, all points are displayed with the same symbol.

- **Categorized**: This is the style of choice if a layer contains points of different categories; for example, a layer containing locations of different animal sightings.

- **Graduated styles**: These are great if we want to visualize numerical values; for example, temperature measurements.

- **Rule-based styles**: These are the most advanced options. These styles are very flexible because they allow us to write multiple rules for one layer.

- **Point displacement styles**: These are only available for point layers. These styles are useful if you need to visualize point layers with multiple points at the same coordinates; for example, students of a school living at the same address.

Below the drop-down list we find the symbol preview, and below that there is the list of symbol layers, which shows us the different layers the symbol consists of. On the right-hand side, we find options for the symbol size and size units, color and transparency, as well as rotation. Using the **Data defined properties** button, we can also tell QGIS to use the feature's attribute values to define symbol shape, size, color, and so on. Finally, the bottom-right area contains a preview area with saved symbols.

Point layers are by default displayed using a simple circle symbol. We want to use a symbol of an airplane instead. To change the symbol, select the **Simple marker** entry in **Symbol layers**. Notice how the right-hand side of the dialog changes. We can now see the options available for simple markers: **Colors**, **Size**, **Rotation**, **Form**, and so on. However, we are not looking for circles, stars, or square symbols—we want an airplane. That's why we need to change the **Symbol layer type** option from **Simple marker** to **SVG marker**. Many of the options are similar, but on the bottom we now find a selection of SVG images that we can choose from. Scroll through the list and pick the airplane symbol as shown in the following screenshot:

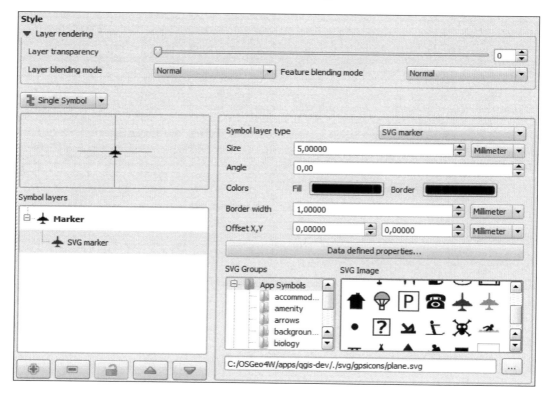

Symbol layer types for point layers include the following:

- **Simple marker**: These include geometric forms such as circles, stars, and squares

- **Font marker**: These provide access to your symbol fonts

- **SVG marker**: Each QGIS installation comes with a collection of default SVG symbols; add your own folders containing SVG images by going to **Settings** | **Options** | **System** | **SVG Paths**

- **Ellipse marker**: These include customizable ellipses, rectangles, crosses, and triangles; especially useful when combined with what we set in the data defined settings option

- **Vector Field marker**: This is a customizable vector-field visualization tool

Creating line styles – an example of river or road styles

In this exercise, we will create a river style for the `majriver.shp` file in our sample data. The goal is to create a line style with two colors: a fill color for the center of the line and an outline color. This technique is very useful because it can also be used to create road styles.

To create such a style, we combine two simple lines. The default symbol is one simple line. Click on the green **+** symbol located below the **Symbol layers** list to add another simple line. The lower one will be our outline and the upper one will be the fill. Select the upper simple line and change the color to blue and the width to 0.3 millimeters. Next, select the lower simple line and change its color to gray and the width to 0.6 millimeters, slightly wider than the other line. Check the preview and click on **Apply** to test how the style looks when applied to the river layer.

You will notice that the style doesn't look perfect yet. That's because each line feature is drawn separately, one after the other, and this leads to a rather disconnected appearance. Luckily, that's easy to fix; we only need to enable the so-called symbol levels. To do that, select the **Line** entry in the **Symbol layers** list and tick the checkbox in the **Symbol Levels** dialog of the **Advanced** section (the button in the lower-right corner of the style dialog) as shown in the following screenshot. Click on **Apply** to test the results:

Whenever we create a symbol that we might want to re-use in other maps, we can save it by going to **Symbol | Save in symbol library** (the button beside the **Advanced** button in the bottom-right corner). We can assign a name to the new symbol; after we save it, it will be added to the **Saved styles** preview area.

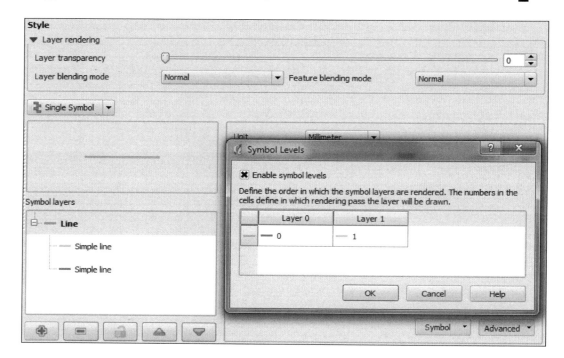

Symbol layer types for line layers include the following:

- **Simple line**: These are solid or dashed lines
- **Marker line**: These lines are made out of point markers located at line vertices or in regular intervals

Creating polygon styles – an example of a landmass style

In this exercise, we will create a style for the `alaska.shp` file. The goal is to create a simple fill with a blue halo. Like in the previous river style example, we will combine two symbol layers to create this style: a simple fill layer that defines the main fill color with a thin border and an additional simple line outline layer for the halo. The halo should have nice rounded corners. To achieve those, change the **Join style** option to **Round**. Similar to the previous example, we again enable symbol levels; to prevent this landmass style from blocking out the background map, we select the **Multiply** blending mode as shown in the following screenshot:

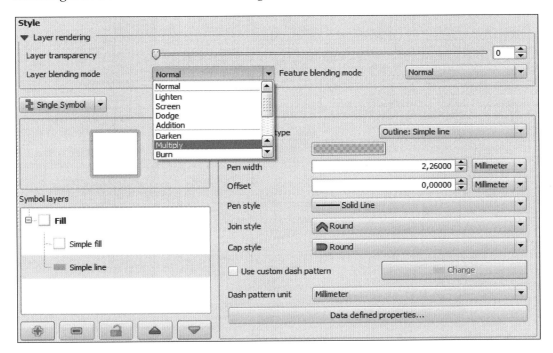

Symbol layer types for polygon layers include the following:

- **Simple fill**: These define fill and outline colors as well as basic fill styles
- **Centroid fill**: These allow us to put point markers at the center of polygons
- **Line/Point pattern fill**: These support user-defined line and point patterns with flexible spacing
- **SVG fill**: These fill the polygon using SVG patterns
- **Outline**: These make it possible to outline areas using line styles

Loading background maps

Background maps are very useful for quick checks and to provide orientation, especially if you don't have access to any other base layers. Adding background maps is easy using the OpenLayers plugin. It provides access to satellite, street, and hybrid maps by Google, Yahoo!, and Bing, as well as different map types by OpenStreetMap, Stamen, and Apple.

To install the OpenLayers plugin, go to **Plugins | Manage and Install Plugins | Get more**. Wait until the list of available plugins has finished loading. Use the filter to look for the **OpenLayers Plugin** option as shown in the following screenshot. Select it from the list and click on **Install**. This is going to take a moment. Once it's done, you will see a short confirmation message. You can then close the installer and the **OpenLayers Plugin** option should be available through the **Plugins** menu.

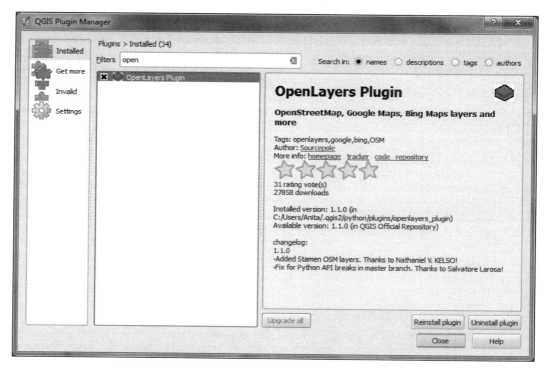

Note that you have to be online to use these services. Another fact worth mentioning is that all these services provide their maps only in Pseudo Mercator (EPSG:3857). Your project CRS will automatically be changed to Pseudo Mercator when you load a background map using the **OpenLayers plugin** option.

If you load the OSM Landscape layer, your map will look like the following screenshot:

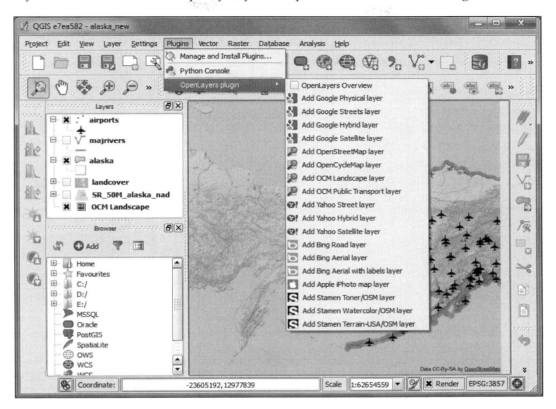

Summary

In this chapter, we covered how to load spatial data from files, databases, and web services. We saw how QGIS handles coordinate reference systems and had a first introduction to styling vector and raster layers, a topic we will cover in more detail in *Chapter 5, Creating Great Maps*. We also installed our first Python plugin, the OpenLayers plugin, and used it to load background maps into our project.

Data Creation and Editing

In this chapter, we will first create some new vector layers and cover how to select features and take measurements. We will then continue with editing feature geometries and attributes. Then, we will reproject vector and raster data, and before we end this chapter, learn how to convert between different file formats with joining data from text files and spreadsheets to our spatial data.

Creating new vector layers

In this exercise, we'll create a new layer from scratch. QGIS offers a wide range of functionalities to create different layers. The **Layer | New** menu lists functions to create new Shapefile and SpatiaLite layers, but we can also create new database tables using the DB Manager plugin. The interfaces differ slightly to accommodate the features supported by each format.

Let's create a new Shapefile to see how it works. A new Shapefile layer, which can be accessed by going to **Layer | New** or *Ctrl + Shift + N*, opens the New Vector Layer dialog with options for different geometry types, CRS, and attributes. The process itself is really fast because all mandatory fields already have default values. By default, it will create a new point layer with WGS84 CRS (unless specified otherwise in **Settings | Options | CRS**) and one integer field called **id**. We can simply click on **OK**, specify a filename, and a new layer appears in the layer list.

Next, we also create one line and one polygon layer. We'll add some extra fields to these layers. Besides integer fields, Shapefiles also support text and decimal values. To add a field, we only need to insert a name, select a type and width, and click on **Add to attributes list**. For decimal numbers, we also have to define the **Precision** value, which determines the number of digits after the comma. A **Width** value of **3** with a **Precision** value of **1** will allow a value range from -99.9 to + 99.9. The following screenshot shows the **New Vector Layer** dialog and the **Attributes...** window for my example polygon layer:

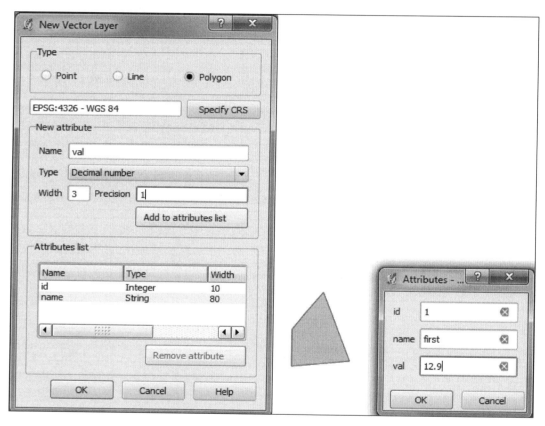

All of the new layers are empty so far, but we will create some features now. If we want to add features to a layer, we first have to enable editing for this layer. Editing can be turned on and off by selecting **Layer | Toggle editing**, **Toggle editing** in the layer name context menu, or with the **Toggle editing** button in the **Digitizing** toolbar. Notice how the layer's icon in the layer list changes to reflect whether editing is on or off. When we turn on editing for a layer, QGIS automatically enables the digitizing tools suitable for the layer's geometry type.

Now, we can use the **Add Feature** tool in the editing toolbar to create new features. To place a point, we simply click on the map. We are then prompted to fill out the attribute form, and once we click on **OK** the new feature is created. Like with points, we can create new lines and polygons by placing nodes onto the map. To finish a line or a polygon, we simply right-click on the map. Create some features in each layer and then save your changes. We can re-use these test layers in the upcoming exercises.

 New features and feature edits are saved permanently only after clicking on the **Save Layer Edits** button in the **Digitizing** toolbar or once we finish editing and confirm that we want to save.

Working with feature selection tools

Selecting features is one of the core functions of any GIS, and it is useful to know them before we venture forward into editing geometries and attributes. Depending on the use case, selection tools come in many different flavors. QGIS offers three different kinds of tools to select features using the mouse, an expression, or another layer.

The first group of tools in the **Attributes** toolbar allows us to select features on the map using the mouse, either one at a time or by drawing different shapes such as rectangles or freehand areas around the features. All features that intersect with the drawn shape are selected. Holding down *Ctrl* will add the new selection to an existing one.

Similarly, holding down *Ctrl + Shift* will remove the new selection from the existing selection. The following screenshot shows the tools:

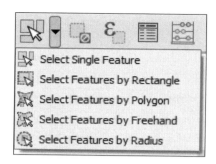

The second type of select tool is called **Select by Expression** and it is also available in the **Attribute** toolbar. It selects features based on expressions that can contain references and functions using feature attributes and/or geometry. The list of available functions is pretty long, but we can use the search box to filter the list by name to find the function we are looking for faster. On the right-hand side of the window, we find the **Selected Function Help**, which explains the functionality and how to use the function in an expression. The **Function List** also shows the layer attribute fields, and by clicking on **Load all unique values** or **Load 10 sample values**, we can easily access their content. Like with the mouse tools, we can choose between creating a new selection or adding to or deleting from an existing selection. Additionally, we can choose to only select features from within an existing selection. Let's have a look at some example expressions that you can build on and use in your own work:

- Using the lakes.shp file in our sample data, we can, for example, select big lakes with an area bigger than 1,000 square miles using a simple attribute query: "AREA_MI" > 1000.0, or by using geometry functions such as $area > (1000.0 * 27878400). Note that the lakes.shp CRS uses feet and we therefore have to multiply by 27,878,400 to convert from square feet to square miles.

- We can also work with string functions, for example, to find lakes with long names: length("NAMES") > 12, or lakes with names that contain an "s" or "S": lower("NAMES") LIKE '%s%', which first converts the names to lower case and then looks for any appearance of "s". The dialog will look like the following screenshot:

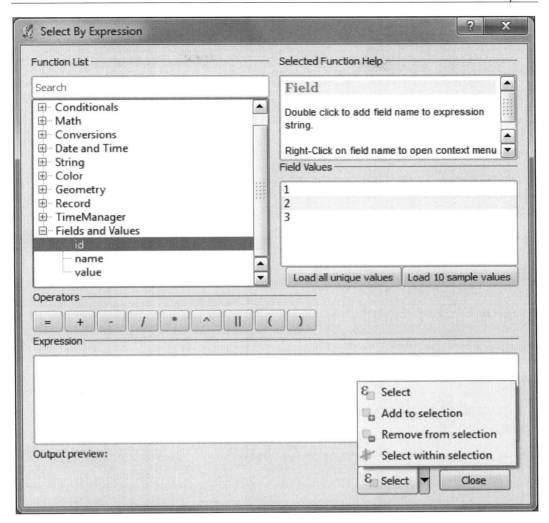

The third type of tool allows us to select features in one layer based on their location relative to features in a second layer. These tools can be accessed by going to **Vector | Research Tools | Select by location** and **Vector | Spatial Query | Spatial Query**. Enable it in **Plugin Manager** if you cannot find it in the **Vector** menu. In general, we want to use the Spatial Query plugin as it supports a variety of spatial operations such as **crosses**, **equals**, **intersects**, **is disjoint**, **overlaps**, **touches**, and **contains** depending on the layer geometry type.

Let's test the Spatial Query plugin using `railroads.shp` and `pipelines.shp` from the sample data. For example, we might want to find all the railroad features that cross a pipeline; we therefore select the **railroads** layer, the **Crosses** operation, and the **pipelines** layer. After clicking on **Apply**, the plugin presents us the query results. There is a list of IDs of the result features on the right-hand side of the window as you can see in the following screenshot. Below this list, we can check the **Zoom to item** checkbox, and QGIS will zoom to the feature that belongs to the selected ID. Additionally, the plugin offers buttons to directly save all the resulting features to a new layer.

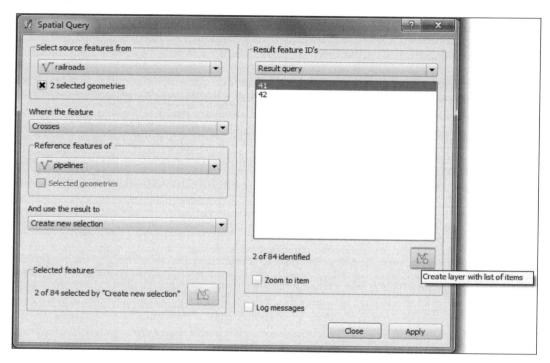

Editing vector geometries

Now that we know how to create and select features, we can have a closer look at the other tools in the **Digitizing** and **Advanced Digitizing** toolbars. The Digitizing toolbar will look like the following screenshot:

The basic **Digitizing** toolbar contains tools for creating and moving features and nodes, as well as for deleting, copying, cutting, and pasting features, as follows:

- With the **Move Feature(s)** tool, it is easy to move one or more features at once by dragging them to the new location.

- Similarly, the **Node Tool** feature allows us to move one or more nodes of the same feature. The first click activates the feature, while the second click selects the node. Hold the mouse key down to drag the node to its new location. Instead of moving only one node, we can also move an edge by clicking and dragging the line. And finally, we can select and move multiple nodes by holding down *Ctrl*.

- **Delete Selected**, **Cut Features**, and **Copy Features** are only active if one or more layer features are selected. Similarly, **Paste Features** only works after a feature has been cut or copied.

The **Advanced Digitizing** toolbar offers very useful **Undo** and **Redo** functionalities as well as additional tools for more involved geometry editing:

- **Rotate Feature(s)** enables us to rotate one or more selected features around a central point.

- Using the **Simplify Feature** tool, we can simplify/generalize feature geometries by simply clicking on the feature and pulling the tolerance slider in the pop-up window.

- The following tools allow us to **Add Rings**, also known as "holes", into existing polygons or **Add Parts** to existing polygons. And of course, there are tools to **Delete Rings** and **Delete Parts** as well.

- **Reshape Features** can be used to alter the geometry of a feature by either cutting out or adding pieces. You can control the behavior by starting to draw the new form inside the original feature to add a piece, or start outside to cut out a piece, as shown in the following example diagram:

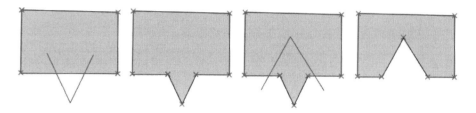

- The **Offset Curve** tool is only available for lines and allows us to displace a line geometry by a given offset.
- **Split Features** allows us to cut one or more features along a cut line.
- **Merge Selected Features** enables us to merge multiple features while keeping control over which feature's attributes will be available in the output feature.
- Similarly, **Merge Attributes of Selected Features** lets us combine the attributes of multiple features, but without merging them into one feature. Instead, all original features remain as they were, but the attribute values are updated.
- Finally, **Rotate Point Symbols** is only available for point layers with the **Rotation field** feature enabled (which we will cover in *Chapter 5, Creating Great Maps*).

Using the measuring tools

Another core functionality of any GIS are the measurement tools. In QGIS, we find tools to measure lines, areas, and angles in the **Attribute** toolbar, as shown in the following screenshot:

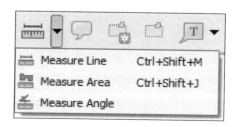

The measurements are updated continuously while we draw measurement lines, areas, or angles. When we draw a line with multiple segments, the tool will show the length of each segment as well as the total length of all the segments put together. To stop measuring, we just right-click. If we want to change the measurement units from meters to feet or from degrees to radians, we can do that in **Settings** | **Options** | **Map Tools**.

Editing attributes

There are three main use cases for attribute editing. First, we might want to edit the attributes of one specific feature, for example, to fix a wrong name. Second, we might want to edit attributes of a group of features. Or third, we might want to change the attributes of all the features within a layer. All these use cases are covered by functionality available through the attribute table. We can access it by going to **Layer** | **Open Attribute Table**, the **Open Attribute Table** button present in the **Attributes** toolbar, or in the layer name context menu.

To change attribute values, we always have to first enable editing. Then we can double-click on any cell in the attribute table to activate the input mode. Clicking on *Enter* confirms the change, but to save the new value permanently, we have to also click on the **Save Edit(s)** button or press *Ctrl + S*. In the bottom-right corner of the attribute table dialog, we can switch from the table to the form view, as shown in the following screenshot, and start editing there.

Another option for editing the attributes of one feature is to open the attribute form directly by clicking on the feature on the map using the **Identify tool**. By default, the **Identify tool** displays the attribute values in the read mode, but we can enable **Open feature form if a single feature is identified** by going to **Settings | Options | Map Tools**.

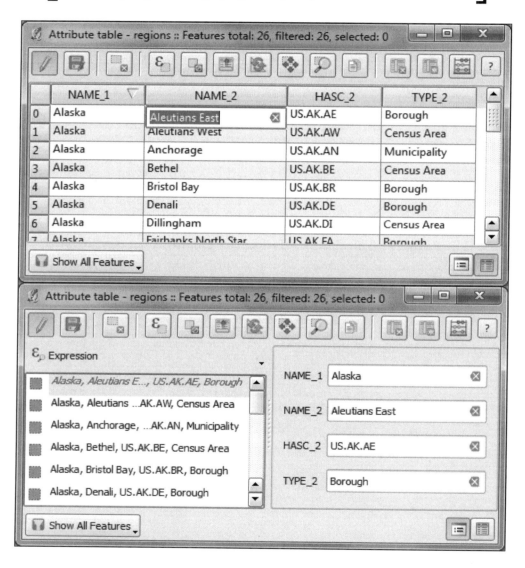

In the attribute table, we also find tools to handle selections (from left to right starting at the third button): Delete selected features, Select by expression, Cancel the selection, Move selected features to the top of the table, Invert the selection, Pan to the selected features, Zoom to the selected features, and Copy the selected features. Another way to select features in the attribute table is to click on the row number.

The next two buttons allow us to add and remove columns. When we click on the delete column button, we get a list of columns to choose from. Similarly, the add columns button brings up a dialog to specify the name and data type of the new column.

If we want to change attributes of multiple or all features in a layer, editing them manually usually isn't an option. That is what **Field Calculator** is good for. We can access it using the **Open field calculator** button in the attribute table or using the *Ctrl + I* keys. In **Field Calculator**, we can choose to only update selected features or to update all the features in the layer. Besides updating an existing field, we can also create a new field. The function list is the same one we already explored when we selected features by expression. We can use any of these functions to populate a new field or update an existing one. Here are some example expressions that are used often:

- We can create an id column using the $rownum function, which populates a column with the row numbers as shown in the following screenshot
- Another common use case is to calculate line length or polygon area using the geometry functions $length and $area respectively
- Similarly, we can get point coordinates using $x and $y

- If we want to get the start or end points of a line, we can use `xat(0)` and `yat(0)` or `xat(-1)` and `yat(-1)`

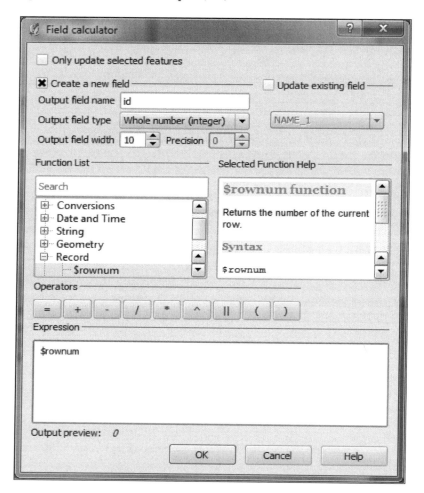

Reprojecting and converting vector and raster data

In *Chapter 2*, *Viewing Spatial Data*, we talked about CRS and the fact that QGIS offers on-the-fly reprojection to display spatial datasets, which are stored in different CRS, in the same map. Still, in some cases, we will want to permanently reproject a dataset, for example to geoprocess it later on.

In QGIS, reprojecting a vector or raster layer is done by simply saving it with a new CRS. We can save a layer using **Layer | Save as ...** or **Save as ...** in the layer name context menu. Pick a target file format and file name, and then click on the **Browse** button besides the CRS field to pick a new CRS.

Besides changing the CRS, the main use case of the Save vector/raster layer dialog is to convert between different file formats. For example, we can load a Shapefile and export it as GeoJSON, Mapinfo MIF, CSV, and so on, or the other way around.

The Save raster layer dialog is also a convenient way to clip/crop rasters by a bounding box, as we can specify which extent we want to save.

Similarly, for vector layers, there is **Save selection as ...** in both the **Layer** menu and the layer name context menu, which will open the same kind of dialog, but it will only save the selected features.

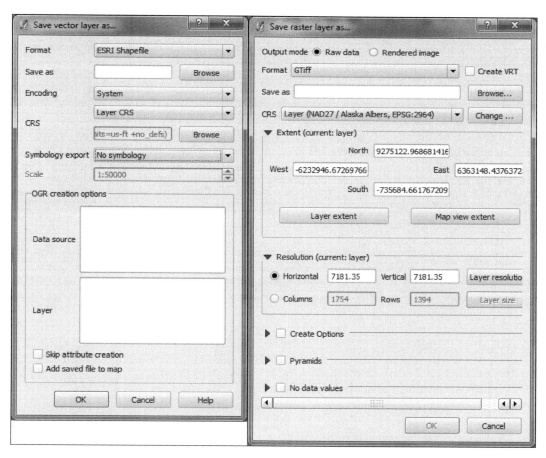

> Enabling **Add saved file to map** (currently only available in the vector dialog) is very convenient because it saves us the effort to go and load the new file manually after it has been saved.

Joining tabular data

In many real-life situations, we get additional non-spatial data in the form of spreadsheets or text files. The good news is we can load XLS files by simply dragging them into QGIS from the file browser or using **Add Vector Layer**. Don't let the wording fool you! It really works without any geometry data in the file. The file can even contain more than just one table. You will see the following dialog, which lets you choose which table(s) you want to load:

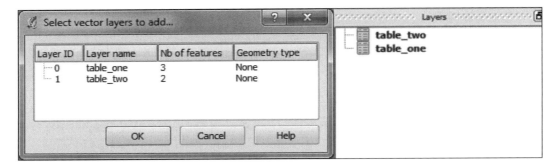

QGIS will automatically recognize the names and data types of columns in an XLS table. It's quite easy to tell because numeric values are right-aligned in the attribute table as shown in the following screenshot:

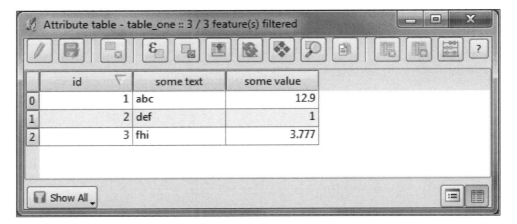

We can also load tabular data from delimited text files like we saw in *Chapter 2, Viewing Spatial Data*, when we loaded a point layer from a delimited text file. To load a delimited text file that only contains tabular data but no geometry information, we just need to enable the **No geometry** (attribute table only) option.

After loading the tabular data from either the spreadsheet or text file, we can continue to join this non-spatial data to a vector layer. To do that, we go to the vector **Layer Properties | Joins** tab. There, we can add a new join by pressing the green plus button. All we have to do is select the tabular **Join layer** and **Join field** fields (of the tabular layer), which should contain values that match those in the **Target field** field (of the vector layer). The page will look like the following screenshot.

 The way joins work in QGIS is that the join layer's attributes are appended to the original layer's attribute table. The number of features in the original layer is not changed. Whenever there is a match between the join and the target field, the attribute value will be filled; otherwise you'll see NULL entries.

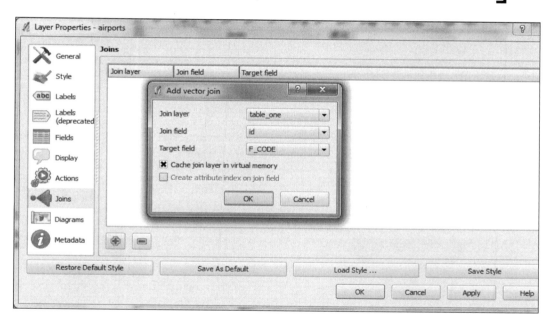

Once the join is added, we can see the extended attribute table and use the new appended attributes for styling and labeling.

You can save the joined layer permanently. Just use
Save as ... to create the new file.

Summary

In this chapter, we covered how to create new layers from scratch. We used the tools to create and edit feature geometries in different ways. Then, we went into editing feature attributes of single features, feature selections, and whole layers. Next, we reprojected both vector and raster layers and also learned how to convert between different file formats. Finally, we finished this chapter on layer creation and editing by covering tabular data, how it can be loaded into QGIS, and how to join it to our spatial data.

In the following chapter, we will put our data to good use and learn how to perform different kinds of spatial analysis on raster and vector data.

4
Spatial Analysis

In this chapter, we will start with raster processing and analysis tasks such as clipping and terrain analysis. We will cover the essentials of converting between raster and vector formats, and then continue with common vector geoprocessing tasks such as generating heatmaps and calculating area shares within a region. We will finish the chapter with an introduction to automating geoprocessing workflows using the QGIS Processing modeler.

Clipping rasters

A common task in raster processing is clipping a raster with a polygon. This task is well covered by the Clipper tool located in **Raster | Extraction | Clipper**. This tool supports clipping to a specified extent or clipping using a polygon mask layer, as follows:

* The extent can be set manually or by selecting it in the map. To do that, we just drag open a rectangle in the map area of the main QGIS window.

* A mask layer can be any polygon layer that is currently loaded in the project or any other polygon layer, which can be specified using **Select…**.

> If we only want to clip a raster to a certain extent (the current map view extent or any other), we can also use the raster **Save as …**, as shown in *Chapter 3, Data Creation and Editing*.

For a quick exercise, we will clip the hillshade raster using the Alaska Shapefile (both from our sample data) as a mask layer. At the bottom of the window, we can see the concrete **gdalwarp** command that QGIS uses to clip the raster. This is very useful if you also want to learn how to use GDAL.

The default **No data value** is **0**, but we can override it if necessary. Another good option is to **Create an output alpha band**, which will set all areas outside the mask to transparent, as shown in the following screenshot:

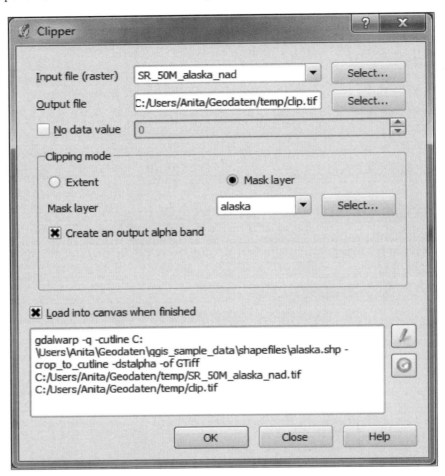

The resulting layer will be loaded automatically since we enabled the **Load into canvas when finished** option. QGIS should also automatically recognize the alpha layer we created, and the raster areas that fall outside the Alaska land mass should be transparent. If, for some reason, QGIS fails to automatically recognize the alpha layer, we can enable it manually using the **Transparency band** option in the raster layer properties' **Transparency** section. This dialog is also the right place to specify any **No data value** we want to be used, as shown in the following screenshot:

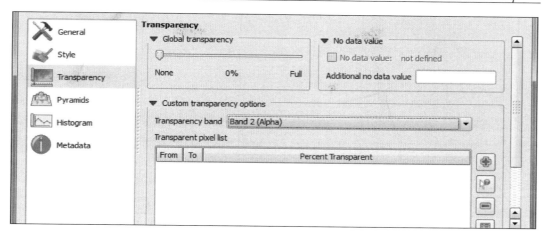

Analyzing elevation / terrain data

Raster terrain analysis can be used to calculate the slope, aspect, hillshade, ruggedness index, and relief from elevation rasters, as shown in the following screenshot. These tools are available through the **Raster | Terrain analysis** plugin, which comes with QGIS by default, but we have to enable it in the Plugin Manager.

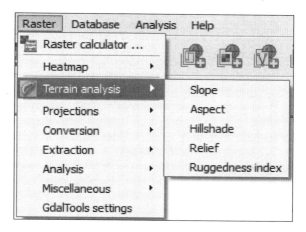

The Terrain analysis includes the following tools:

- **Slope**: This tool calculates the slope angle for each cell in degrees (based on the first order derivative estimation)
- **Aspect**: This tool calculates the exposition (in degrees counter-clockwise, starting with 0 for north)
- **Hillshade**: This tool creates a basic hillshade raster with lighted areas and shadows
- **Relief**: This tool creates a shaded relief map with varying colors for different elevation ranges
- **Ruggedness Index**: This tool calculates the ruggedness index for each cell by summarizing the elevation changes within a 3 x 3 cell grid

Of course, to use any of these terrain analysis tools, we need an elevation raster. If you don't have any at hand, you can simply download a dataset from the NASA **Shuttle Radar Topography Mission (SRTM)** using http://dwtkns.com/srtm/ or any of the other SRTM download services.

 If you want to replicate the results in the following exercise exactly, please get the dataset called srtm_05_01.zip, which covers a small part of Alaska.

An important element in all terrain analysis tools is the **Z factor**. The z factor is used if the x/y units are different from the z (elevation) unit. For example, if we tried to create a relief from elevation data where x/y are in degrees and z is in meters, the resulting relief would look grossly exaggerated. The values for the z factor are as follows:

- If x/y and z are either all in meters or all in feet, use the default z factor 1.0
- If x/y are in degrees and z is in feet, use the z factor 370,400
- If x/y are in degrees and z is in meters, use the z factor 111,120

Since the SRTM rasters are provided in WGS84 EPSG:4326, we need to use a **Z factor** of 111120 in our exercise. Let's create a relief! The tool can calculate relief color ranges automatically; we just need to click on **Create automatically**, as shown in the following screenshot. Of course, we can still edit the elevation ranges' upper and lower bounds, as well as the colors.

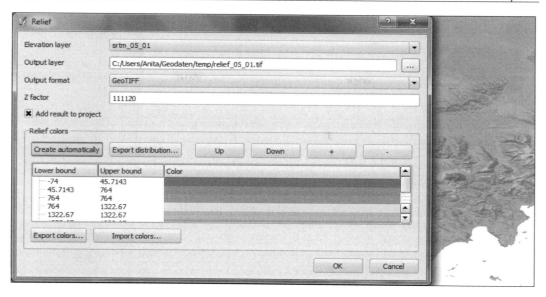

While relief maps are three-banded rasters, which are primarily used for visualization purposes, slope rasters are a common intermediate step in spatial analysis workflows. We will now create a slope raster, which we can use in our example workflow through the following sections. The resulting slope raster will be loaded in grayscale automatically, as shown in the following screenshot:

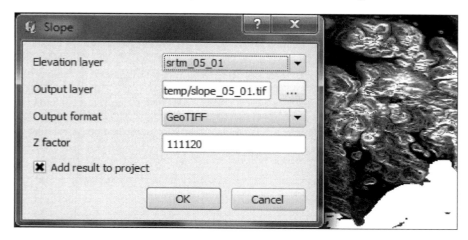

Raster calculator

By going to **Raster | Raster Calculator**, we can create a new raster layer based
on values in one or more rasters that are loaded in the current QGIS project. All
available raster bands are presented in a list in the top-left corner of the dialog in
the form `raster_name@band_number` as shown in the following screenshot.

Continuing from our previous exercise in which we created a slope raster, we can,
for example, find areas at elevations above 1,000 meters and with a slope of less
than 5 degrees using the following expression (you might have to adjust the values
depending on the dataset you are using):

```
srtm_05_01@1 > 1000 AND slope_05_01@1 < 5
```

Cells that meet both criteria of high elevation and evenness will be assigned a value
of 1 in the resulting raster, while cells that fail to meet a criterion will be set to 0. The
only bigger areas with a value of 1 are found in the southern part of the raster layer.

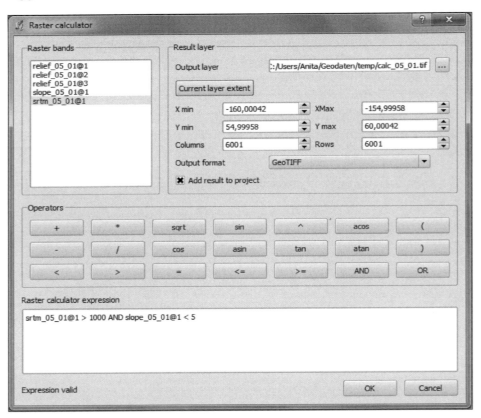

Another typical use case is reclassifying a raster. For example, we could want to reclassify the landcover raster in our sample data so that all areas with a landcover class from 1 to 5 get the value 100, areas from 6 to 10 get 101, and areas over 11 get a new value of 102. We will use the following code for this:

```
( landcover@1 > 0 AND landcover@1 <= 6 ) * 100
+ ( landcover@1 >= 7 AND landcover@1 <= 10 ) * 101
+ ( landcover@1 >= 11 ) * 102
```

The preceding raster calculator expression has three parts, consisting of a check and a multiplication. For each cell, only one of the three checks can be true, and true is represented as 1. Therefore, if a landcover cell has a value of 4, the first check will be true and the expression evaluates to `1*100 + 0*101 + 0*102 = 100`.

Converting between rasters and vectors

Tools for converting between raster and vector formats are available in **Raster | Conversion** and are called Rasterize and Polygonize. Like the raster clipper tool we used before, this tool is also based on GDAL and displays the command at the bottom of the dialog.

Polygonize converts a raster into a polygon layer; depending on the size of the raster, the conversion can take some time. When the process is finished, QGIS will notify us with a pop up. For a quick test, we can, for example, convert the reclassified landcover raster to polygons. The resulting vector polygon layer contains multiple polygon features with a single attribute we called `lc`, which depends on the original raster value, as shown in the following screenshot:

The Rasterize tool is very similar to the Polygonize tool. The only difference is that we get to specify the size of the resulting raster in pixels/cells. We can also specify the attribute field, which will provide input for the raster cell value. The **cat** attribute of our `alaska.shp` dataset is rather meaningless, but you get the idea of how the tool works, as shown in the following screenshot:

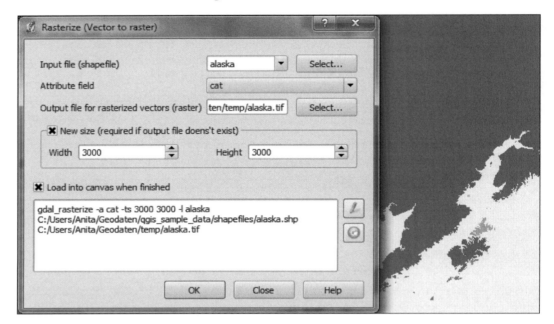

Accessing raster and vector layer statistics

Whenever we get a new dataset, it is useful to examine the layer statistics to get a feeling for the data. Raster layer statistics are readily available in the **Layer Properties** dialog, specifically in the following tabs:

- **Metadata** shows the minimum and maximum cell value as well as the mean and the standard deviation
- **Histogram** presents the distribution of raster values
- For vector layers, we can get summary statistics using two tools in **Vector | Analysis Tools**:

○ **Basics statistics** is very useful for numeric fields. It calculates parameters such as mean and median, min and max, the feature count *n* and the number of unique values, and so on for all the features of a layer or for the selected features only.

○ **List unique values** is useful to get all the unique values of a certain field.

In both the tools, we can easily copy the results using *Ctrl + C* and paste them into a text file or spreadsheet. The following screenshots show examples exploring the contents of our airport sample dataset:

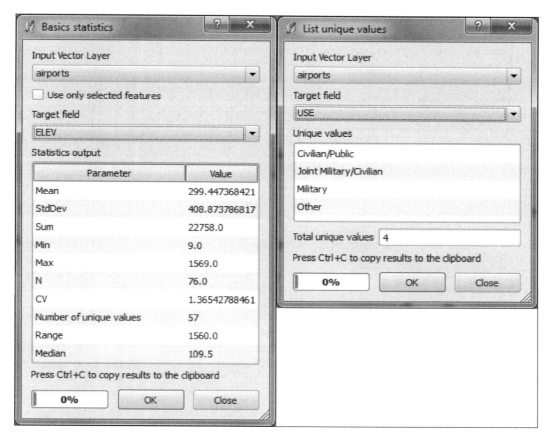

Creating a heatmap from points

Heatmaps are great for visualizing the distribution of points. To create them, QGIS provides a simple to use **Heatmap Plugin**, which we have to activate in **Plugin Manager**, and then we can access it by going to **Raster | Heatmap | Heatmap**. The plugin offers different kernel shapes to choose from and allows us to control the raster size in cells as well as the cell size. The **Heatmap Plugin** looks like the following screenshot:

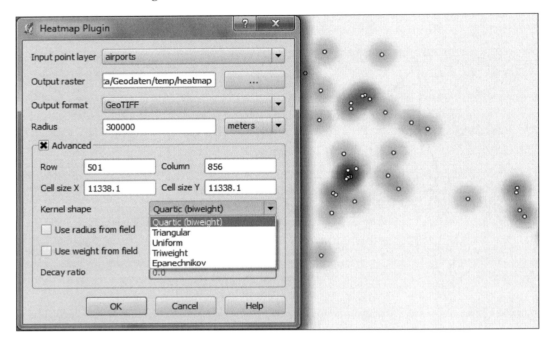

Vector geoprocessing with Processing

The most comprehensive set of spatial analysis tools is accessible via the Processing plugin, which we can also enable in **Plugin Manager**. When the plugin is enabled, we find an **Analysis** menu where we can activate the toolbox, as shown in the following screenshot. In the toolbox, it is easy to find spatial analysis tools by their name thanks to the dynamic search box at the top. This makes finding tools in the toolbox easier than in the vector or raster menu. Another advantage of getting accustomed to the Processing tools is that they can be automated in Python and in geoprocessing models.

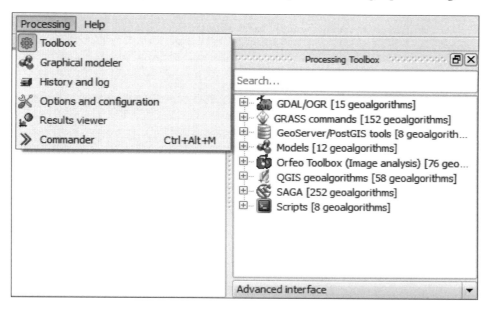

Note that the preceding screenshot shows the advanced interface of the toolbox. You can switch from the simplified interface to the advanced interface using the drop-down button at the bottom of the toolbox. I prefer using the advanced version as it exposes all available algorithms and clearly displays how individual tools are related to the different components such as GDAL/OGR or GRASS.

In the following sections, we will cover a selection of the available geoprocessing tools and see how we can use the modeler to automate our tasks.

Identifying features in the proximity of others

One common spatial analysis task is to identify features in the proximity of certain other features. One example would be to find all the airports near rivers. Using `airports.shp` and `majrivers.shp` from our sample data, we can find airports within 5,000 feet of a river using a combination of the **Fixed distance buffer** and **Select by location** tools, as shown in the following screenshot:

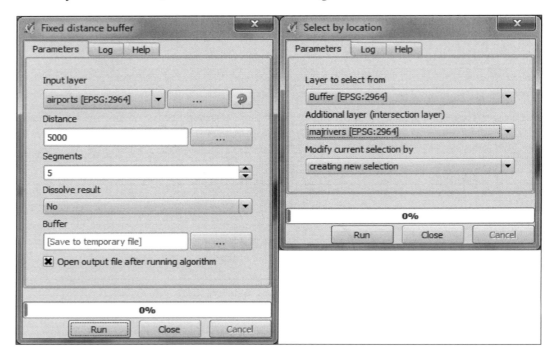

After buffering the airport point locations, the **Select by location** option selects all the airport buffers that intersect a river. As a result, 14 out of the 76 airports are selected. This information is displayed in the information area at the bottom of the QGIS main window as shown in the following screenshot:

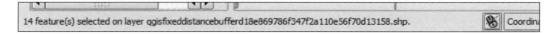

If you ever forget which settings you used or need to check that you used the correct input layer, you can go to **Analysis | history and log**. The **ALGORITHM** section lists all the algorithms we have been running as well as the used settings. This is also the right place to look for error messages in the **WARNING** section, as shown in the following screenshot:

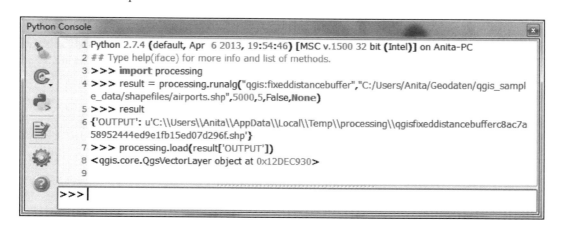

The commands listed under **ALGORITHM** can also be used to call Processing tools from the QGIS Python console by going to **Plugins | Python Console**. The Python commands shown in the following screenshot run the buffer algorithm and load the result into the map:

Raster sampling at point locations

Another common task is to sample a raster at specific point locations. Using Processing, we can solve this problem using a GRASS tool called v.sample. To use GRASS tools, make sure GRASS is installed and Processing is configured correctly in **Analysis | options and configuration**. On an OSGeo4W default system, the configuration will look like the following screenshot:

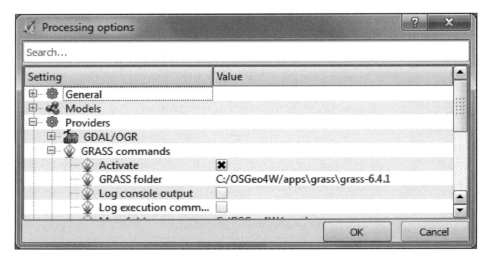

For this exercise, let's imagine we want to sample the landcover layer at the airport locations of our sample data. All we have to do is specify the vector layer containing the sample points and the raster layer that should be sampled. For this example, we can leave all other settings to their defaults. The tool will not only sample the raster, it also compares point attributes with the sampled raster value, but we don't need this comparison in our current example.

The dialog will look like the following screenshot:

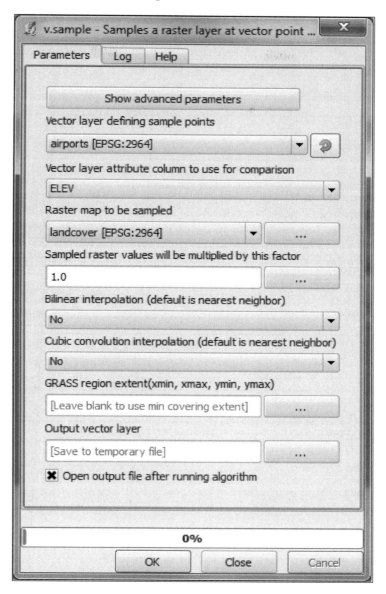

Mapping density with hexagonal grids

Mapping the density of points using a hexagonal grid has become a quite popular alternative to creating heatmaps. Processing offers us a fast way to create such an analysis. There is already a pre-made script called **Hex grid from layer bounds**, which we can use to first create a hexagonal grid that covers all points in the input layer. The dataset of populated places, popp.shp, is a good sample dataset for this exercise. Once the grid is ready, we can run **Count points in polygon** to calculate the statistics. In case you cannot see the resulting layer, go to the **Layer Properties | General** tab and make sure the **CRS** field is set to **NAD 27 / Alaska Albers**. The tools dialog will look like the following screenshot:

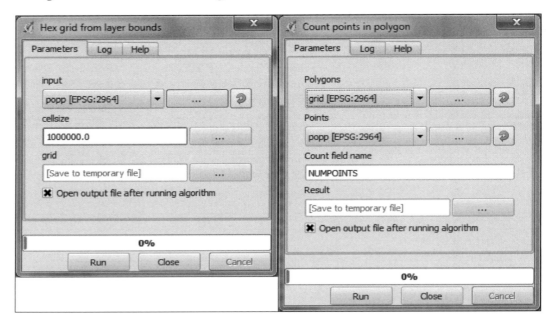

Calculating area shares within a region

Another spatial analysis task we often encounter is calculating area shares within a certain region, for example, landcover shares along one specific river. Using `majrivers.shp` and `trees.shp`, we can calculate the share of wooded area in a 5,000 feet strip of land along the `Susitna River` value parameter. We first define the analysis region by selecting the river and buffering it. Note that the **Dissolve result** option should be set to **Yes** to ensure that the buffer result is one continuous polygon, as shown in the following screenshot.

 QGIS Processing will only apply buffers to the selected features of the input layer. This default behavior can be changed in **Analysis | options and configuration** by disabling the **Use only selected features** option.

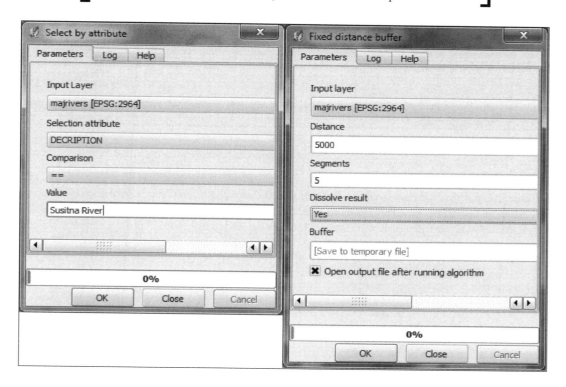

Next, we calculate the size of the strip of land around our river. This can be done using the **Export/Add geometry columns** tool, which adds the area and parameter to the attribute table. Then we can calculate the **Intersection** field between the area along the river and the wooded areas in `trees.shp`, as shown in the following screenshot:

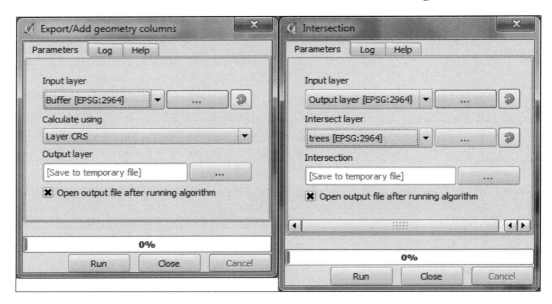

Using the **Dissolve** tool, we can recombine all areas from the intersection results into one big polygon representing the total wooded area around the river. Finally, we can calculate the final share of wooded area using **Advanced Python field calculator**. The formula `value = $geom.area()/<area>` divides the area of the final polygon (`$geom.area()`) by the value in the "area" attribute (`<area>`), which we created in a previous step by running **Export/Add geometry columns**. The tools will appear as shown in the following screenshot:

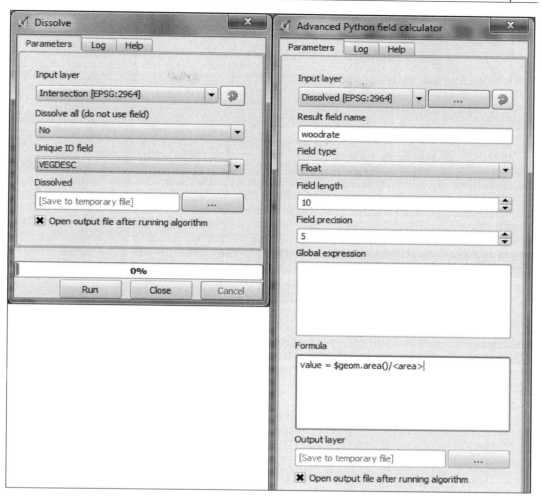

This calculation results in a wood share of 0.31601 for **Deciduous** and 0.09666 for **Mixed** trees. Therefore, we can conclude that in total, 41.27 percent of the land along Susitna River is wooded.

Automated geoprocessing with the graphical modeler

Using the graphical modeler, we can turn whole geoprocessing and analysis workflows into automated models. To create a model, we go to **Analysis | Graphical modeler** to open the modeler where we can select from different **Inputs** and **Algorithms** for our model.

Let's create a model that automates the creation of hexagonal heatmaps! By double-clicking on the **Vector layer** entry in the **Inputs** list, we can add an input field for the point layer. It's a good idea to use descriptive parameter names so we can recognize which input is first and which is later in the model. It is also useful to restrict the **Shape type** field where appropriate. In our example, we restrict the input to **Point**. This will enable Processing to prefilter the available layers and present us only with layers of the correct type. The second input we need is a **Number** field to specify the desired hexagonal cell size. The tool will look like the following screenshot:

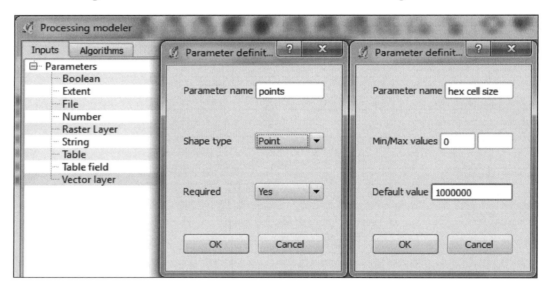

After adding the inputs, we can now continue creating the model by assembling the algorithms. In the **Algorithms** section, we can use the filter at the top to narrow down our search for the correct algorithm. To add an algorithm to the model, we simply double-click on the entry in the list of algorithms. This opens the algorithm dialog where we have to specify the inputs and further algorithm-specific parameters.

In our example, we want to use the point vector layer as the **input** layer, and the number input **hex cell size** as the **cellsize** parameter. We can access the available inputs through the drop-down list. Alternatively, it's also possible to hardcode parameters such as the cell size.

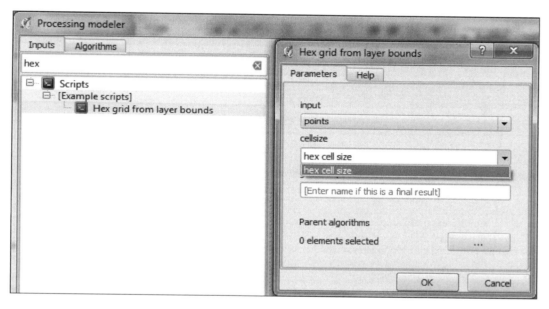

While adding the following algorithms, it is important to always choose the correct **input** layer based on the previous processing step. We can verify the correct workflow using the arrow connections in the model diagram that the **modeler** draws automatically. The tool will look like the following screenshot:

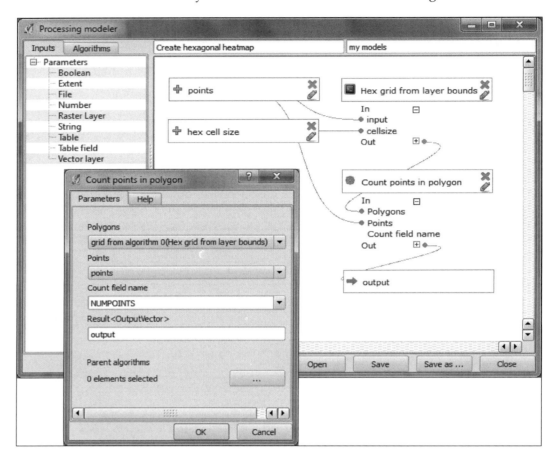

To finish the model, we should enter a model name (for example, `Create hexagonal heatmap`) and a group name (for example, `my models`). Processing will use the group name to organize all the models we create. Once we have picked a name and group, we can save the model and then run it. After closing the modeler, we can run the saved models from the toolbox like any other tool. It is even possible to use one model as a building block in another model.

Another useful feature is that we can specify a layer style, which should be applied to the processing results automatically. This default style can be set using **Edit rendering styles for outputs** in the context menu of the created model in the toolbox, as shown in the following screenshot:

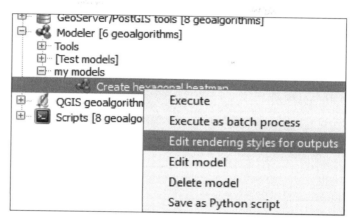

Summary

In this chapter, we covered various raster and vector geoprocessing and analysis tools and how to apply them in common tasks. We saw how to use the Processing toolbox to run individual tools as well as the modeler to create complex geoprocessing models from multiple tools. Using the modeler, we can automate our workflows and increase our productivity, especially with respect to reoccurring tasks.

In the following chapter, we will learn how to bring all our knowledge together to create beautiful maps using advanced styles and map compositioning features.

5
Creating Great Maps

In this chapter, we will cover the important features that enable us to create great maps. We will first go into advanced vector styling, building on what we learned in *Chapter 2, Viewing Spatial Data*. Then, we will learn how to label features by following examples for point labels as well as more advanced road labels with road shield graphics. We will also cover how to tweak labels manually. Finally, we will get to know the print composer and how to use it to create printable maps and map books.

Advanced vector styling

This section introduces more advanced vector styling features, building on the basics we saw in *Chapter 2, Viewing Spatial Data*. We will see how to use graduated styles, categorized styles, and rulebased styles.

Creating a graduated style with size-scaling

Graduated styles are great to visualize distributions of numeric values in a choropleth map or similar. In our sample data, there is a `climate.shp` file, which contains locations and mean temperature values that we can visualize using a graduated style by simply selecting the value **T_F_MEAN** for the **Column** field and clicking on **Classify**. We can pick an existing **Color ramp** field or create a new one by scrolling down the list to the **New color ramp...** entry. Graduated styles are available in different classification modes as follows:

- **Equal Intervals**: This mode creates classes by splitting at equal intervals between the maximum and minimum values found in the specified column

- **Quantile (Equal Count)**: This mode creates classes so that each class contains an equal number of features

- **Natural Breaks (Jenks)**: This mode uses the Jenks Natural Breaks algorithm to create classes by taking the distribution of values into account

- **Standard Deviation**: This mode uses the column values' standard deviation to create classes

- **Pretty Breaks**: This mode is the only classification that doesn't strictly create the specified number of classes, but tries to find pretty class breaks instead

Besides using color to distinguish between the different temperature values, we can also use size. By setting the **Size scale field** field in the **Advanced** tab to **T_F_MEAN**, as shown in the following screenshot, all point symbols will be scaled so that locations with higher mean temperatures are displayed with a bigger symbol.

 Using **Size scale field**, we can make the size of point symbols or the width of line symbols responsive to a certain attribute value. Note that we can choose between scaling the area or the diameter of a point symbol depending on the nature of the values. Similarly, there is also a **Rotation field** option, which allows us to rotate point symbols. The expected input is in degrees from 0 to 360 with 0 pointing towards the north.

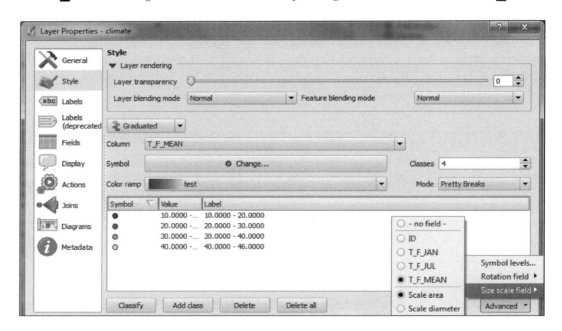

The following screenshot shows the results of using a **Graduated renderer** option with four classes using the **Pretty Breaks** classification mode and a **Size scale field** option, as shown in the preceding screenshot:

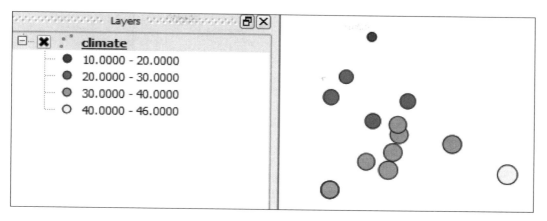

Using categorized styles

Just as graduated styles are very useful to visualize numeric values, categorized styles are great for text values, or more generally speaking, for all kinds of values on a nominal scale. A good example for this kind of data can be found in the `trees.shp` file in our sample data. For each area, there is a **VEGDESC** value that describes the type of forest found there. Using a categorized style, we can very easily generate a style with one symbol for every unique value in the **VEGDESC** column as shown in the following screenshot.

Of course, every symbol is editable and can be customized. Just double-click on the symbol preview to open the **Symbol** selector dialog, which allows us to select and combine different symbols.

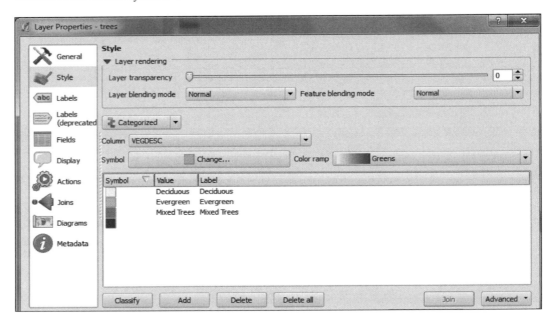

Once we click on **OK**, the style is applied to our trees layer to visualize the distribution of different tree types in the area. The map will look like the following screenshot:

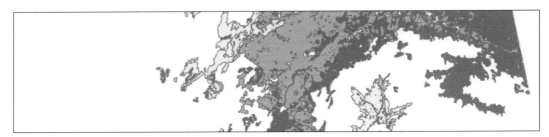

Creating a rule-based style for road layers

With rule-based styles, we can create a layer style with a hierarchy of rules. Rules can take into account anything, from attribute values to scale and geometry properties such as area or length. The following screenshot shows an example of a rule-based renderer for the ne_10m_roads.shp file from Natural Earth (you can download it from http://www.naturalearthdata.com/downloads/10m-cultural-vectors/roads/). On the first level of rules, we distinguish between roads of **"type" = 'Major Highway'** and those of **"type" = 'Secondary Highway'**. The next level of rules handles scale-dependence. To add this second layer of rules, we can use the **Refine current rules** button and select **Add scales to rule**. We simply input one or more scale values at which we want the rule to be split.

There are no symbols specified on the first rule level. If we would have symbols specified on the first level as well, the renderer would draw two symbols over each other. While this can be useful in certain cases, we don't want this effect now. Symbols can be deactivated in the Rule properties, which are accessible by double-clicking on the rule or clicking on the edit button below the rule's tree view (the button between the plus and minus buttons).

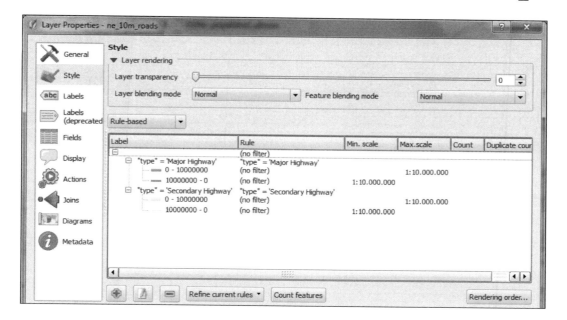

In the following screenshot, we can see the scale rules in action. While the left-hand side shows a simplified version with thin grey lines for secondary highways, the right-hand side version shows wider, white roads with grey outlines.

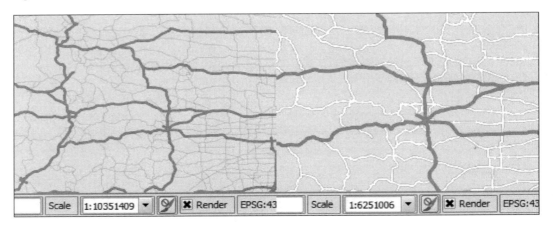

You can download the symbols used in this style by going to **Settings | Style Manager | Share | Import from**. The URL is `https:// raw.github.com/anitagraser/QGIS-resources/master/ symbols/osm_symbols.xml`. Paste the URL in the **Location** textbox, click on **Fetch Symbols**, then on **Select all**, and finally on **Import**. The dialog will look like the following screenshot:

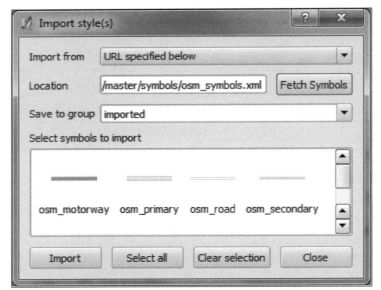

Labeling

We can activate labeling by going to **Layer Properties** | **Labels**, checking **Label this layer with**, and selecting the attribute field that we want to use for the labels. This is all we need to do to display labels with default settings. While default labels are great for a quick preview, we usually want to customize the labels if we create visualizations for reports or stand-alone maps.

Using **Expressions** (the button that is right beside the attribute drop-down list), we can format the label text to suit our needs. For example, the **NAME** field in our sample `airports.shp` file contains text in uppercase. To display the airport names in mixed case instead, we can set the expression `title(NAME)`, which will reformat the name text in title case. We can also use multiple fields to create the label, for example, combining name and elevation in brackets using the concatenation operator || as follows:

```
title(NAME) || ' (' || "ELEV" || ')'
```

Note the use of simple quotation marks around text such as ' (' and double quotation marks around field names such as "ELEV". The dialog will look like the following screenshot:

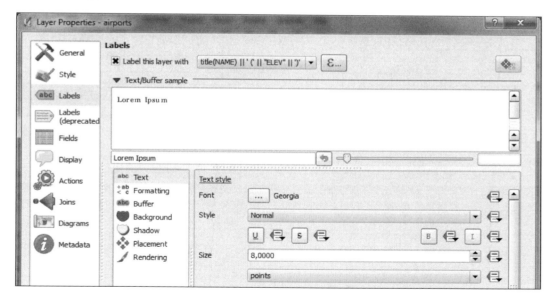

The big preview area at the top of the dialog titled **Text/Buffer sample** shows a preview of the current settings. The background color can be adjusted to test readability on different backgrounds. Under the preview area, we find the following different label settings:

- **Text**: Besides changing the font style, size, color, and transparency, we can also modify letter and word spacing as well as the blend mode, which works like the layer blending mode we covered in *Chapter 2, Viewing Spatial Data*. Note the column of buttons on the right-hand side of every setting. Clicking on these buttons allows us to create so-called data-defined overrides. These can be used, for example, to define different label colors or to vary label size depending on an individual feature's attribute value or an expression.

- **Formatting**: Here we can enable multiline labels by specifying which characters to wrap on. Additionally, we can control **line height** and **alignment**. We can also add a symbol that displays the line's digitizing direction to the label. Finally, the **Formatted numbers** option offers a shortcut to format numeric values to a certain number of decimal places.

- **Buffer**: We can adjust the buffer size, color and transparency, as well as the pen join style, and blending mode. With transparency and blending, we can improve label readability without blocking out the underlying map too much.

- **Background**: This allows us to add a background shape in the form of a rectangle, square, circle, ellipsoid, or an SVG. SVG backgrounds are great to create effects such as highway shields.

- **Shadow**: This makes it possible to add a shadow to labels. We can control everything from shadow direction to color, blur, size, and transparency.

- **Placement**: The available automatic label placement options depend on the layer geometry type. For point layers, we can choose between the following:

  - The flexible **Around point** option tries to find the best position for labels by distributing them around the points without overlaps. As you can see in the following screenshot, some labels are put to the upper-right corner of their point symbol while others appear at different positions in the lower-left (for example, **Anchorage Intl (129)**) or lower-right (for example, **Merrill Fld (123)**) corners.

  - The **Offset from point** option forces all labels to a certain position; for example, all labels can be placed above their point symbol.

The following screenshot shows airport labels with a 50 percent transparent **Buffer** and **Drop Shadow** placed using **Around point** and a **Label distance** of 1 mm:

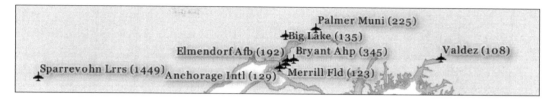

For line layers, we can choose from the following:

- ○ **Parallel** for straight labels that are rotated according to the line orientation
- ○ **Curved** for labels that follow the shape of the line
- ○ **Horizontal** for labels that keep a horizontal orientation regardless of the line orientation

For further fine-tuning, we can define whether the label should be placed **Above line**, **One line**, or **Below line**, and how far above and below using **Label distance**.

The following example shows labels with road shields. You can download a blank road shield SVG from `http://upload.wikimedia.org/wikipedia/commons/c/c3/Blank_shield.svg`. Note how only Interstates are labeled. This can be achieved using the following labeling expression:

```
CASE WHEN "level" = 'Interstate' THEN name END
```

The labels are positioned using the **Horizontal** option. Additionally, **Merge connected lines to avoid duplicate labels** (in the Rendering section) and **Suppress labeling of features smaller than** are activated; for example, 5 mm helps to avoid clutter by not labeling pieces of road that are shorter than 5 mm at the current scale.

To set up the road shield, go to the **Background** section and select the blank shield SVG from the folder you downloaded it to. To make sure that the label fits nicely inside the shield, we additionally specify the **Size type** field as a buffer with a **Size** of 1 mm, which makes the shield a little bigger than the label it contains.

If you click on **Apply** now, you will notice that the labels are not centered perfectly inside the shields. To fix that, we apply a small **Offset** in the **Y** direction to the shield position, as shown in the following screenshot. Additionally, I recommend to deactivate the label **Buffer** as it tends to block out parts of the shield, and we don't need it anyway.

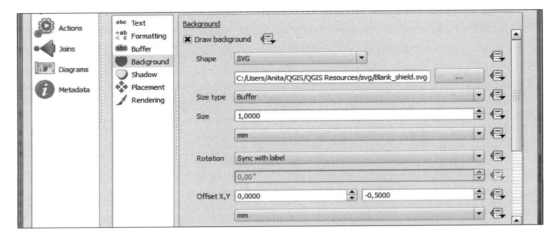

For polygon layers, the options are as follows:

- **Offset from centroid**, which uses the polygon centroid as an anchor and works like **Offset from point** for point layers
- **Around centroid** works in a manner similar to **Around point**
- **Horizontal** places a horizontal label somewhere inside the polygon, independent of the centroid
- **Free** fits a freely rotated label inside the polygon
- **Using perimeter** places the label on the polygon outline

The following screenshot shows lake labels (lakes.shp) using the **Multiple lines** feature wrapping on the empty space character and positioned using the **Free** option:

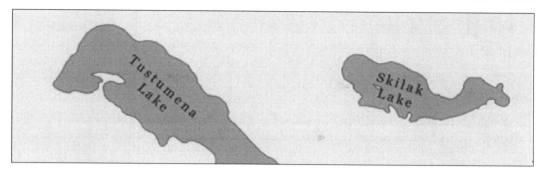

 By default, QGIS avoids overlapping labels, but for debug purposes, it can be useful to force **Show all labels (including colliding labels)** using the options in the Rendering section.

Besides automatic label placement, we also have the option to use data-defined placement to position labels exactly where we want them to be. In the labeling toolbar, we find tools to move and rotate labels by hand. They are only active and available for layers that have data-defined placement for at least X and Y coordinates set up. To start using the tools, we can simply add three new columns, `label_x`, `label_y`, and `label_rot` to, for example, the `airports.shp` file. Then, we can specify these columns in data-defined settings by pressing the buttons beside **Offset X, Y** and **Rotation**. We don't have to enter any values in the attribute table right now. The labeling engine will check for values, and if it finds the attribute fields empty, it will simply place the labels automatically. By specifying data-defined placement, the labeling toolbar's tools are now available (note that the editing mode has to be turned on), and we can use the tools to move and rotate any of the labels on the map. The changes are written back to the attribute table. Try moving some labels, especially where they are placed closely together, and watch how the automatically placed labels adapt to your changes.

- **Rendering**: This allows us to define **scale-based visibility** limits to display labels only at certain scales and **pixel size-based visibility** to hide labels for small features. Here, we can also tell the labeling engine to **show colliding labels,** which are normally hidden by default.

Designing print maps

In QGIS, print maps are designed in the print composer. A QGIS project can contain multiple composers, so it makes sense to pick descriptive names. Compositions are saved automatically whenever we save the project. To see a list of all the compositions available in a project, go to **Project | Composer Manager**.

We can open a new composer by going to **Project | New Print Composer** or by using *Ctrl + P*. The composer window consists of the following:

*   A preview area for the map composition displaying a blank page on start
*   Panels for configuring the **Composition, Item properties**, and **Atlas generation**, as well as a **Command history** panel for quick undo and redo
*   Toolbars for managing, saving and exporting compositions, navigating in the preview area, as well as adding and arranging different composer items

The **Composition** panel gives us access to the paper options such as size, orientation, and number of pages. It is also the place to configure snapping behavior and output resolution.

First, we add a map item to the paper using the **Add new map** button, or by going to **Layout | Add Map** and drawing the map rectangle onto the paper. Click on the paper, keep the mouse button pressed down, and drag the rectangle open. We can move, resize, and zoom the map using the mouse and the **Select/Move item** tools. Alternatively, it is also possible to configure all map settings in the **Item Properties** panel.

The **Item Properties** panel content depends on the currently selected composition item. If a map item is selected, we can adjust the map's **Scale** and **Extents** as well as the **Position and size** tool of the map item itself. At a **Scale** of 10,000,000, we can more or less fit Alaska on an A4 paper. To move the area that is displayed within the map item, we can use the **Move item content** tool.

After the map looks like we want it to, we can add a scale bar using the **Add new scalebar** button or by going to **Layout | Add Scalebar** and clicking on the map. The **Item Properties** panel now displays the scalebar's properties similar to what you can see in the following screenshot. Since we can add multiple map items to one composition, it is important to specify which map the scale belongs to. The second main property is the scalebar style, which allows us to choose between different scalebar types or a **Numeric** type for a simple textual representation such as 1:10,000,000. Using the **Units** properties, we can convert the map units in feet or meters to something more manageable, such as miles or kilometers.

The **Segments** properties control the number of segments and the size of a single segment in the scalebar. Further, the properties control the scalebar's color, font, background, and so on.

North arrows can be added to a composition using the **Add Image** button or by going to **Layout | Add image** and clicking on the paper. It might take a while for the **Item Properties** panel to update while QGIS loads the previews of the images in the SVG folder. Pick a north arrow from the list of images shipped with QGIS or select your own SVG. Further map decorations such as arrows or rectangle, triangle, and ellipse shapes can be added using the appropriate toolbar buttons **Add Arrow**, **Add Rectangle**, and so on.

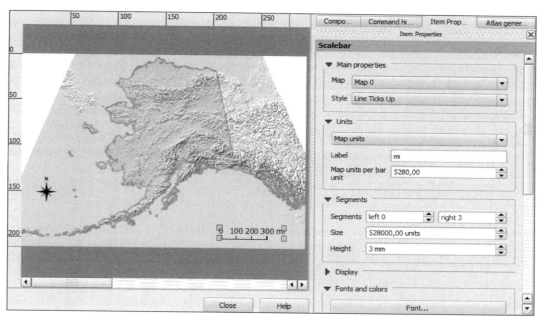

Maps that show an area close up are often accompanied by a second map that tells the reader where the area is located in a larger context. To create such an overview map, we add a second map item and activate its **Overview** option. By setting the **Overview frame**, we can define which detail map's extent should be highlighted.

> Every map item in a composition can display a different combination of layers. Generally, map items in composer are synced with the map in the main QGIS window. So, if we turn a layer off in the main window, it also gets removed from the print composer map. But, we can stop this automatic synchronization by enabling **Lock layers** for a map item in the map item's properties.

Other common map features are grids and coordinate frames. Grids can be enabled for any map item. We can choose between a normal **Solid** grid or **Crosses** only. **Interval** and **Offset** values have to be specified in map units. Additionally, we can activate a value of **Zebra** for the **Frame style** and **Draw coordinates** inside or outside the frame, as shown in the following screenshot:

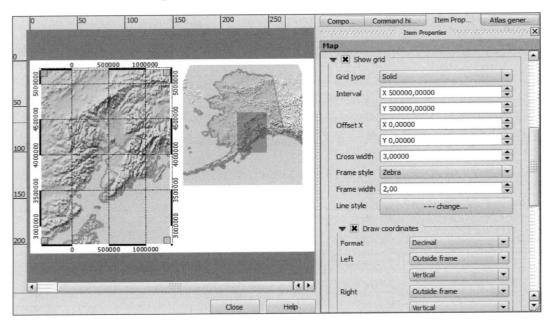

Legends are another vital map element. We can use the **Add new legend** button or go to **Layout | Add legend** to add a default legend with entries for all currently visible map layers. Legend entries can be reorganized, edited, and removed in the Legend items' properties. Using the **Wrap text on** option, we can split long labels on multiple rows as shown in the following screenshot. Additionally, the legend in this example is divided into four columns. By default, QGIS tries to keep all entries of one layer in a single column, but we can override this behavior be enabling **Split layers**.

To add text to the map, we can use the **Add new label** button or go to **Layout | Add label**. Simple labels display all text using the same font. By enabling **Render as HTML**, we can create more elaborate labels with headers, lists, different colors, and highlights in bold or italics using the normal HTML notation, for example:

```
<h1>Alaska</h1>
<p>The name <i>"Alaska"</i> means "the mainland"</p>
<ul><li>one list entry</li><li>another entry</li></ul>
```

Labels can also contain expressions such as:

- [% $now %] to insert the current timestamp
- [% $page %] of [% $numpages %] to insert page numbers in compositions with multiple pages

Even more advanced text areas can be added using the **Add html frame** button. We can point the item's URL reference to any HTML page on our local machines or online, and the content will be displayed on the composer page.

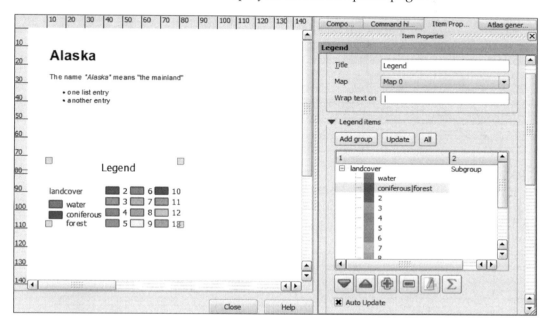

To add additional details to the map, the composer also offers the possibility to add an attribute table to the composition using the **Add attribute table** button or by going to **Layout | Add attribute table**. By enabling **Show only visible features**, we can filter the table and display only relevant results. Sorting and renaming of columns is possible via the **Attributes...** button.

Finally, the **Atlas generation** panel enables us to create a series of maps using one print composition. The tool will create one map for every feature in the **Coverage layer** dropdown we define in the atlas configuration. Features in the Coverage layer can be displayed like regular features or hidden by enabling **Hidden coverage layer**. **Feature sorting** and **Feature filtering** make it possible to further fine-tune the results.

Using the **Fixed scale** option, all maps will be rendered using the same scale. If we need more flexible output, we can switch to the **Margin around feature** option instead, which zooms to every Coverage layer feature and renders it in addition to the specified margin surrounding area. The **Output** field can be one image or PDF for each Coverage layer feature or a multipage PDF by enabling **Single file export** when possible before going to **Composer | Export as PDF**.

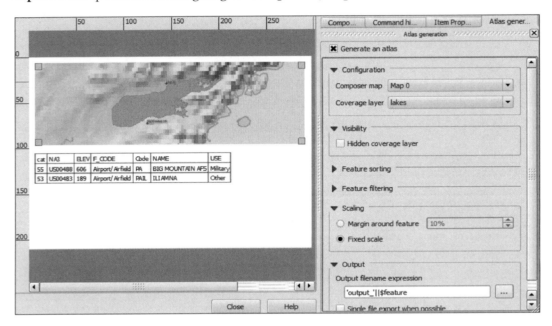

Summary

In this chapter, we had a closer look into how we can create some more complex maps using advanced vector layer styles such as the categorized or rule-based style. We also covered the automatic and manual feature labeling options available in QGIS. This chapter also showed how to create printable maps using print composer, and introduced the Atlas functionality for creating map books. Congratulations! Over the previous chapters, you have learned how to install and use QGIS to create, edit, and analyze spatial data and how to present it in an effective manner.

Index

Thank you for buying
Learning QGIS 2.0

About Packt Publishing

Packt, pronounced 'packed', published its first book "*Mastering phpMyAdmin for Effective MySQL Management*" in April 2004 and subsequently continued to specialize in publishing highly focused books on specific technologies and solutions.

Our books and publications share the experiences of your fellow IT professionals in adapting and customizing today's systems, applications, and frameworks. Our solution based books give you the knowledge and power to customize the software and technologies you're using to get the job done. Packt books are more specific and less general than the IT books you have seen in the past. Our unique business model allows us to bring you more focused information, giving you more of what you need to know, and less of what you don't.

Packt is a modern, yet unique publishing company, which focuses on producing quality, cutting-edge books for communities of developers, administrators, and newbies alike. For more information, please visit our website: www.packtpub.com.

About Packt Open Source

In 2010, Packt launched two new brands, Packt Open Source and Packt Enterprise, in order to continue its focus on specialization. This book is part of the Packt Open Source brand, home to books published on software built around Open Source licences, and offering information to anybody from advanced developers to budding web designers. The Open Source brand also runs Packt's Open Source Royalty Scheme, by which Packt gives a royalty to each Open Source project about whose software a book is sold.

Writing for Packt

We welcome all inquiries from people who are interested in authoring. Book proposals should be sent to author@packtpub.com. If your book idea is still at an early stage and you would like to discuss it first before writing a formal book proposal, contact us; one of our commissioning editors will get in touch with you.

We're not just looking for published authors; if you have strong technical skills but no writing experience, our experienced editors can help you develop a writing career, or simply get some additional reward for your expertise.

Python Geospatial Development

ISBN: 978-1-849511-54-4   Paperback: 508 pages

Build a complete and sophisticated mapping application from scratch using Python tools for GIS development

1. Build applications for GIS development using Python

2. Analyze and visualize Geo-Spatial data

3. Comprehensive coverage of key GIS concepts

4. Recommended best practices for storing spatial data in a database

OpenStreetMap

ISBN: 978-1-847197-50-4   Paperback: 252 pages

Be your own Cartographer

1. Collect data for the area you want to map with this OpenStreetMap book and eBook

2. Create your own custom maps to print or use online following our proven tutorials

3. Collaborate with other OpenStreetMap contributors to improve the map data

4. Learn how OpenStreetMap works and why it's different to other sources of geographical information with this professional guide

Please check **www.PacktPub.com** for information on our titles

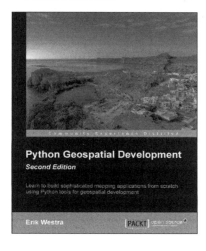

Python Geospatial Development Second Edition

ISBN: 978-1-782161-52-3   Paperback: 508 pages

Learn to build sophisticated mapping applications from scratch using Python tools for geospatial development

1. Build your own complete and sophisticated mapping applications in Python.

2. Walks you through the process of building your own online system for viewing and editing geospatial data

3. Practical, hands-on tutorial that teaches you all about geospatial development in Python

Instant OpenLayers Starter

ISBN: 978-1-782165-10-1   Paperback: 58 pages

Web Mapping made simple and fast!

1. Learn something new in an Instant! A short, fast, focused guide delivering immediate results.

2. Visualize your geographical data

3. Integrate with third party map services to create mash-ups

4. Stylize and interact with your maps

Please check **www.PacktPub.com** for information on our titles

4493990R00061

Made in the USA
San Bernardino, CA
21 September 2013